JERUSALEM
IN THE YEAR 30 A.D.

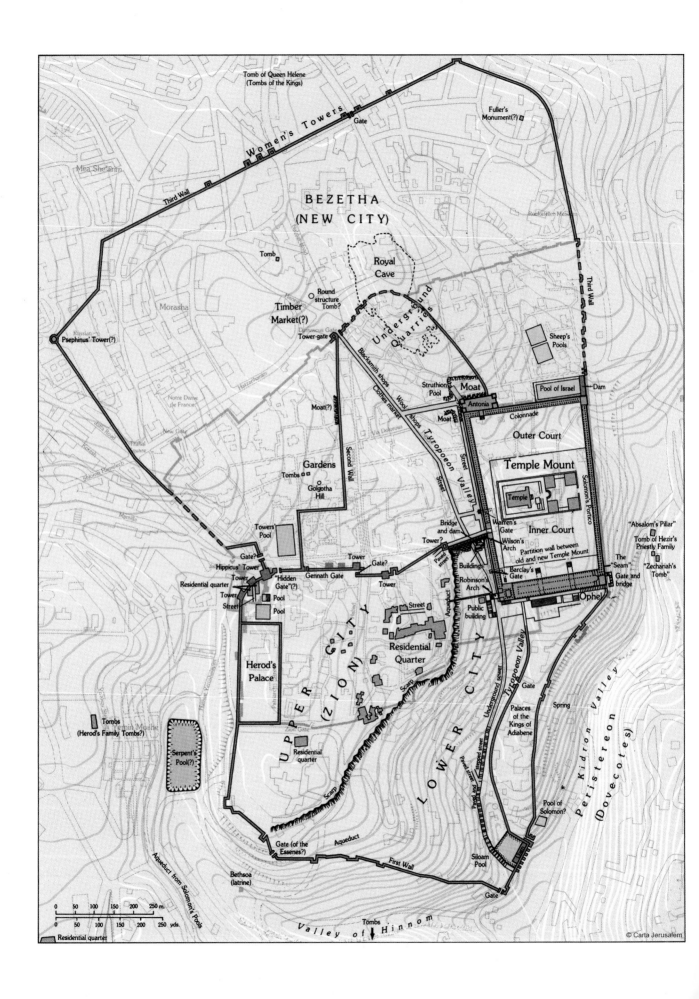

Tomb of Queen Helene
(Tombs of the Kings)

Women's Towers

Gate

Fuller's
Monument(?)

Third Wall

BEZETHA
(NEW CITY)

Mea She'arim

Royal
Cave

Third Wall

Tomb

Morasha

Round
structure
Tomb?

Timber
Market(?)

Underground Quarries

Rockefeller Museum

Sheep's
Pools

Psephinus' Tower(?)

Russian

Damascus Gate
Tower-gate

Struthion
Pool

Moat

Pool of Israel

Dam

Notre Dame
de France

Blacksmith shops

Clothes market

Wool Shops

Antonia

Colonnade

Moat(?)

Via Dolorosa

Shops

Moat

New Gate

Tyropoeon Valley

Outer Court

Gardens

Second Wall

Street

Temple Mount

Tombs

Golgotha
Hill

Temple

Solomon's Portico

Towers'
Pool

Street

Inner Court

"Absalom's Pillar"

Tower

Gate?

Tower

Bridge
and dam

Warren's
Gate

Wilson's
Arch

Partition wall between
old and new Temple Mount

Tomb of Hezir's
Priestly Family

Gate?

Paved
street

Buildings

Barclay's
Gate

The
"Seam"

"Zechariah's
Tomb"

Hippicus' Tower

Gate?

Tower

"Hidden
Gate"(?)

Gennath Gate

Tower

Robinson's
Arch

Gate and
bridge

Residential quarter

Tower
Street

Pool

U
P
P
E
R

C
I
T
Y

Aqueduct

Public
building

Ophel

Pool

Street

Residential
Quarter

Herod's
Palace

Zion Gate

Scarp

L
O
W
E
R

C
I
T
Y

Tyropoeon Valley

Gate

Spring

(
Z
I
O
N
)

Tombs
(Herod's Family Tombs?)

Yemin Moshe

Residential
quarter

Palaces
of the
Kings of
Adiabene

Kidron Valley

Serpent's
Pool(?)

Scarp

Paved street

Underground sewer

Peristereon
(Dovecotes)

Pool of
Solomon?

Gate (of the
Essenes?)

Aqueduct

First Wall

Siloam
Pool

Aqueduct from Solomon's Pools

Bethsoa
(latrine)

Gate

0 50 100 150 200 250 m.

0 50 100 150 200 250 yds.

Tombs

Valley of Hinnom

© Carta Jerusalem

Residential quarter

Leen & Kathleen Ritmeyer

JERUSALEM
IN THE YEAR 30 A.D.

Carta Jerusalem

Second revised edition 2015

Sources
Illustrations by Leen and Nathaniel Ritmeyer:
pp. 7, 9, 10–32, 34–47, 48 (bottom), 49, 50 (bottom), 51–53, 54 (bottom), 55–58,
60, 62–69, 70 (bottom), 71–72
Photograph on p. 14 by Philip Evans
All others Carta Jerusalem

Frontispiece: Map of Jerusalem in the Second Temple Period

Designed and produced by Carta Jerusalem, Ltd.
Editor: Barbara Ball
Artwork: Leen Ritmeyer

ISBN: 978-965-220-856-9

Printed in Israel

CONTENTS

Coin of Herod the Great.

The Temple, the focus of Herod the Great's massive building project, was begun in the 18th year of his reign, in about 19 B.C. The Temple itself was completed in eighteen months and the outer cloisters in eight years. Herod formally dedicated the Temple in 10 B.C. However, construction work must have continued because we read in John's Gospel 2.20 that the Temple had been forty-six years in the making, slightly more than the biblical generation of forty years. This would bring us up to the time of the fifth Roman procurator, Pontius Pilate (26–36 A.D.), when it is recorded that Jesus, with his disciples, beheld the city from the Mount of Olives.

Spread before them was a city which had been utterly transformed during their lifetime. Although Herod had left the scene in 4 A.D., it was only then that his grand design for the city could clearly be seen. Viewed from the east, with the Judean desert behind them, the light and shadows of evening—the time when Jesus retreated to the Mount of Olives after having spent the day in the Temple—played on the splendid buildings with which Herod had adorned the city. Off to the western edge of the Upper City, in the exclusive residential quarter that enjoyed purer air than the Lower City, to the south, there stood the king's own palace, guarded by the three great towers of Mariamme, Phasael and Hippicus. From this spot, the old wall, which he had strengthened with many towers, ran along the upper crest of the Hinnom Valley, across the Tyropoeon which bisected the city, and enclosed the ancient City of David with its densely packed houses. The theater, which he built despite the opposition of his Jewish subjects, stood somewhere in the more liberal milieu of the Upper City.

However, it was the Temple, the crowning glory of all his architectural creations, that drew every eye. True, it was merely a reconstruction of the Second Temple built by the returning exiles from Babylon. Herod had not been permitted by the Jewish religious authorities to make any substantial changes in the Temple building apart from doubling the height of the Porch to bring it into line with the dimensions of the Temple of Solomon. However, in the vast esplanade surrounding it, Herod gave vent to his mania for building. The Temple platform was no longer restricted to Mount Moriah, but doubled in size. In the process many of the surrounding valleys were filled in.

But there, unbelievably close to the Sanctuary, was evidence of Herod's connivance with the occupying power. The Antonia Fortress, at the northwest corner of the Temple platform, stood glowering over the Sanctuary, with a garrison of Roman soldiers to keep watch over Herod's restive subjects.

In front of Herod's Palace, on the second highest peak of the Western Hill, was another palace of magnificent proportions, not built by Herod, but by the Hasmoneans who had preceded him. Herod resided here only until his own palace was completed. The Herodian dynasty, however, still had claims on the former Hasmonean Palace, where Herod's successors stayed on their regular visits to the city.

Close by, to the south, on the brow of the hill, was the palace of the former High Priest Annas, whose office at the time was held by his son-in-law. Across the shimmering expanse of the Temple platform to the northwest was the area of the upper markets, safely enclosed within the Second Wall built by Herod.

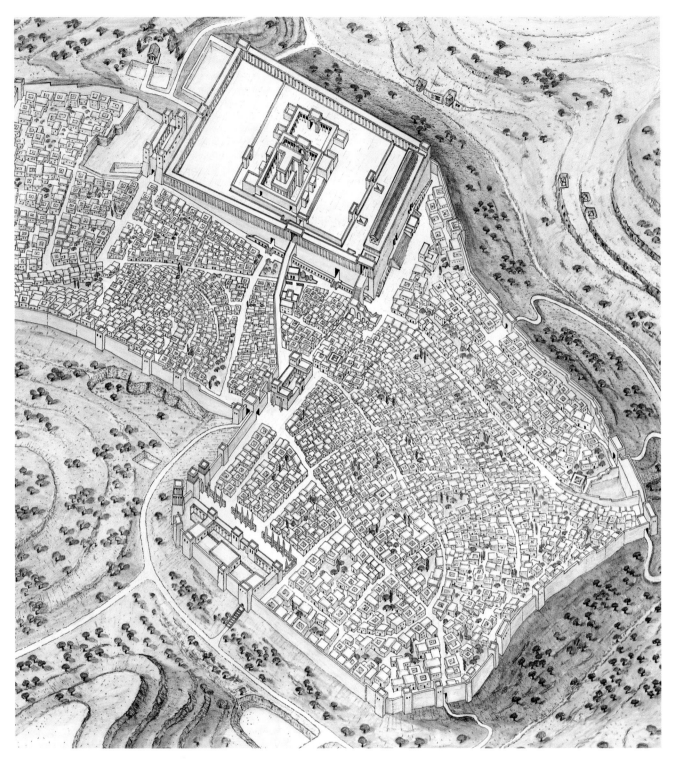

It was the product of a golden age. How strange, therefore, the words of Jesus—"See ye not all these things? Verily I say unto you, There shall not be left one stone upon another that shall not be thrown down" (Matt. 24.2)—must have sounded in the ears of his disciples.

The culmination of King Herod the Great's extravagant plan for Jerusalem. From a city struggling under the Hasmonean dynasty to regain its original boundaries of the First Temple period, Herod created a sophisticated metropolis. Its fame was not restricted to the province of which it was the capital, but in the words of Philo: "Jerusalem was the metropolis not only of Judea but of many other countries" (Delegation to Gaius 281).

Roman bust, thought to be that of Josephus Flavius.

Because of its topography, the outline and scope of first-century Jerusalem is easily recognized in the city two thousand years later.

The three hills—Mount Moriah, the Eastern Hill and the Western Hill—over which the city extended, are still clearly discernible, as are the deep valleys of the Kedron and Hinnom that hold the city, as it were, in the palm of a giant hand. The accumulated debris of centuries has, of course, changed the typography of the city to some extent. The Tyropoeon or Central Valley, which divided Mount Moriah and the Eastern Hill from the Western Hill, is almost completely silted up.

Few cities have been so extensively documented or excavated as has Jerusalem. We are thus provided with a solid framework in which to test the multitude of theories developed by the many researchers who have made the study of ancient Jerusalem their life's work. Outstanding among the written sources are the works of Josephus Flavius, himself a Jerusalemite, born in about 37 A.D. Although prone to exaggeration, his works, *The Jewish War* and *Jewish Antiquities*, provide us with invaluable details as to the configuration of the city at that time. The Mishnah, a collection of tractates dealing with religious and legal matters, compiled about the end of the second century A.D., is valuable for the many references to the city's landmarks, its minute portrayal of life within the city, and its delineation of the Temple layout and ritual in tractates such as *Middot* (measurements) and *Tamid* (daily whole-offering). The contribution of the New Testament in this regard is to flesh out these details and to tie them to a specific period, i.e., the third decade of the first century A.D.

For 1,800 years, the disasters that periodically struck the city caused increasing damage to the city walls and landmarks, until the new science of archaeology turned the tables. Instead of Jerusalem's glory being progressively buried, it was brought to light.

Edward Robinson, the American biblical scholar, blazed the trail in 1838 with his meticulous topographical survey of the city. Then followed the landmark explorations of Charles Warren between the years 1867 and 1870, under the auspices of the Palestine Exploration Fund, which produced an invaluable set of plans and sections. Since then, independent scholars and schools of archaeology worldwide have continued to uncover the city's past. Following the Six-Day War in 1967, unprecedented opportunities opened up. Israeli archaeologists planned systematic excavations with precise objectives in mind. This reconstruction drawing is a synthesis of these results, with other details culled from the the written sources.

The writings of Josephus inform us that from the eastern cloisters of the Temple Mount, the First Wall ran above the Kedron Valley, including in its fortifications the "tower which lieth out" of Nehemiah's time and another tower which can be clearly dated to the Hasmonean period. The wall of a large dam belonging to the Siloam reservoir was also part of the city wall, after which it ran along the southern slopes of

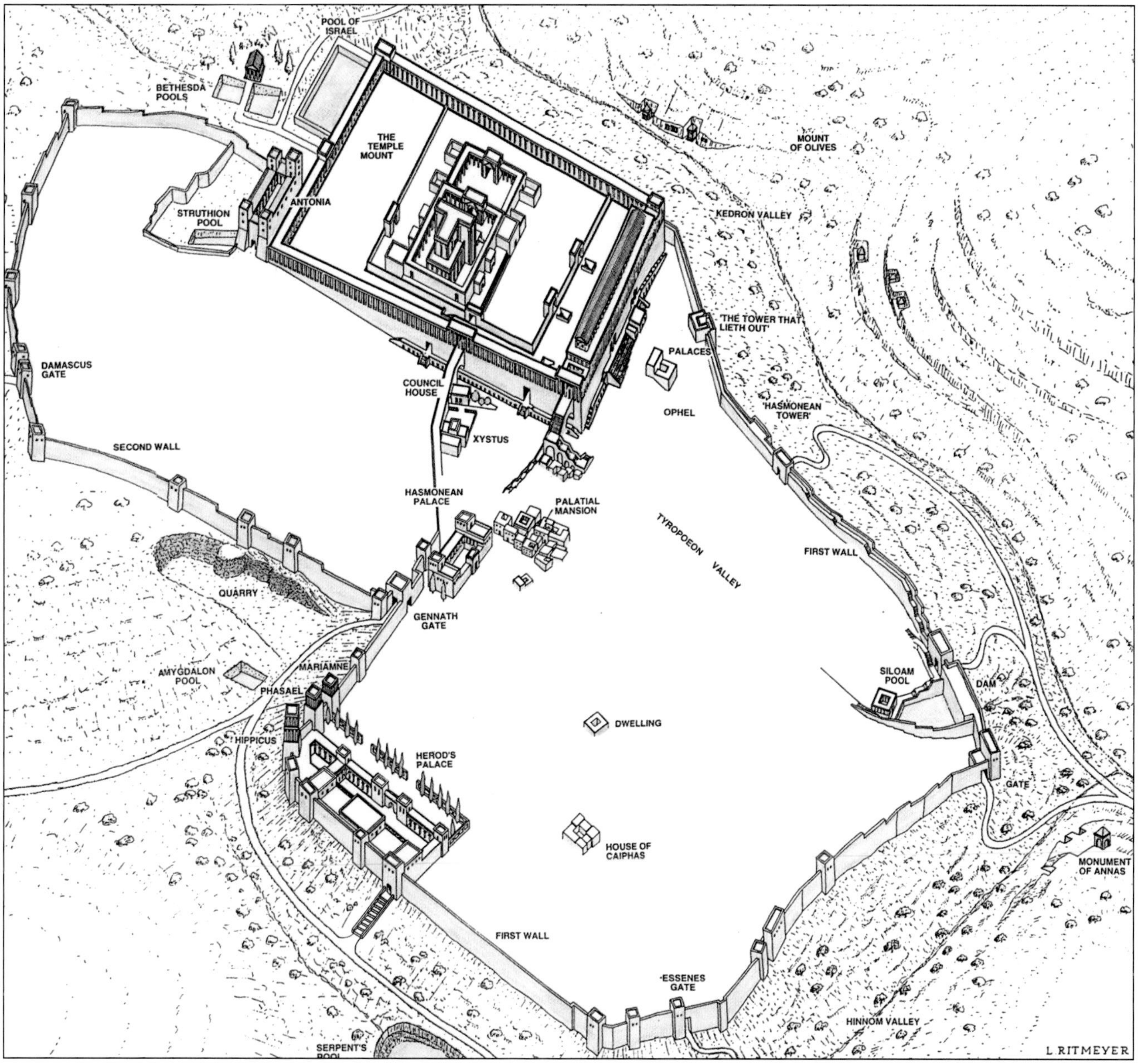
POOL OF ISRAEL
BETHESDA POOLS
THE TEMPLE MOUNT
MOUNT OF OLIVES
ANTONIA
STRUTHION POOL
KEDRON VALLEY
'THE TOWER THAT LIETH OUT'
PALACES
DAMASCUS GATE
COUNCIL HOUSE
OPHEL
'HASMONEAN TOWER'
XYSTUS
SECOND WALL
HASMONEAN PALACE
PALATIAL MANSION
TYROPOEON VALLEY
FIRST WALL
QUARRY
GENNATH GATE
SILOAM POOL
DAM
MARIAMNE
AMYGDALON POOL
PHASAEL
DWELLING
HIPPICUS
HEROD'S PALACE
GATE
HOUSE OF CAIPHAS
MONUMENT OF ANNAS
FIRST WALL
ESSENES GATE
HINNOM VALLEY
SERPENT'S
L RITMEYER

the Western Hill, linking up with the Gate of the Essenes. It then curved round to meet up with the outer wall of Herod's Palace, incorporating the three great towers of Hippicus, Phasael and Mariamme. From there it veered in the direction of the western portico of the Temple Mount, passing the Hasmonean Palace, the Xystus (the former Gymnasium) and the Council Chamber.

The line of the Second Wall is less clear. Our main source, Josephus, records merely that it began at the Gennath Gate in the First Wall and ended at the Antonia Fortress, which stood at the northwest corner of the Temple Mount. Its construction is believed to date from the Hasmonean or early Herodian period. We shall justify our positioning of the wall in due course, when we proceed to examine the various features of the city, point by point. It is indeed the walls that present the most difficult questions.

Other major features such as Herod's Palace and the Council Chamber are fairly well attested. No remains of the Hasmonean Palace have come to light, despite the fact that its location can be accurately surmised. The various pools and water reservoirs have been found just where they were to be expected. And, although the exact mode of the development of the Temple Mount is contested, there is unanimity among scholars that the Temple Mount of Herod stood on the eastern ridge, dominating the city just as it does today.

Sultan Suleiman the Magnificent, from a 19th century engraving. The walls surrounding the Old City today date from his reign.

(right) The Temple Mount today, viewed from the Mount of Olives. Taking the large rectangular building on the left, the King David Hotel, as a point of reference, we will trace the extent of the city enclosed by the Second Wall. In between the hotel and the golden Dome of the Rock, we see the top of the Hippicus Tower, one of the three towers Herod had constructed to defend his palace. This marked the western boundary of Herodian Jerusalem. Now to the Church of the Redeemer, which is the white tower visible between the Dome of the Rock and the Plaza Hotel—the

The view from the Mount of Olives across the Kedron Valley shows the dominant architectural feature of Jerusalem—the Temple Mount. It has remained so from the period of King Solomon, the builder of the First Temple, down to the present day. Even through centuries of appalling neglect, its sheer size and strategic position could not be ignored. As in the past, the present-day city rises beyond the Temple Mount towards the higher Western Hill of Jerusalem. The recently gilded Islamic shrine of the Dome of the Rock is now the jewel in the crown. The only part of the city wall visible is the eastern wall. This wall, the most ancient of the outer retaining walls of the Temple Mount, is the only wall whose line remained unchanged in Herod's massive extension of the Temple platform. The foundations of the central portion of this wall date back to the First Temple period.

The upper courses and crenellations were added during the reign of Suleiman the Magnificent in the sixteenth century A.D. During the Second Temple period there was an eastern gate, called the Shushan Gate, on the site of what is known today as the Golden Gate.

After the destruction of the city by Titus in 70 A.D. and the construction of a Roman colony, Aelia Capitolina, by Hadrian in 132 A.D., the city decreased in size. The city walls of today are partly based on the Hadrianic city wall that roughly followed the line of the Second Wall. Remnants of the first-century city wall are still visible in today's cityscape.

(above) A view of the excavations near the southern wall of the Temple Mount, covered in snow.

highest building on the horizon in the center of the photograph. From the white tower of the Church of the Redeemer, the city wall ran to the right in the direction of the Church of the Holy Sepulchre, marked by the gray dome close to the horizon. From the Church of the Holy Sepulchre the wall ran north (right in the picture) towards the area of the Damascus Gate, which is outside the picture. From there, it went back again towards the Antonia Fortress, where the tall minaret just below the highest building on the horizon in the right of the picture (the Holiday Inn) now stands.

THE TEMPLE MOUNT OF KING HEROD

The Temple Mount at the time of King Herod. The dimensions of the Temple Mount were as follows: northern wall—1,035 feet (315 m), southern wall—912 feet (278 m), eastern wall—1,536 feet (468 m) and western wall—1,590 feet (485 m). These walls are still a prominent feature in this area of Jerusalem.

The Temple Mount was the hub of this great city. King Herod had a passion for building and a desire to emulate the vast Oriental-Hellenistic sanctuaries of Heliopolis and Palmyra then under construction. He was not above building temples to the pagan gods in non-Jewish cities like Sebastia, in Samaria. Here in Jerusalem, however, he was limited to enlarging the height of the Temple Porch to its original Solomonic dimensions, embellishing the Temple's exterior, and extending the platform on which it stood, all of which he undertook with great vigor.

On very uncertain ground because of his Edomite background, Herod had to be careful not to antagonize his Jewish subjects and promised that there would be no interruption in the Temple service. He had all the materials prepared in advance, one thousand wagons to carry the stones, and ten thousand highly skilled workmen in his employ. A thousand priests had become stone masons or carpenters and were given special training for these sensitive tasks. We can envisage the daily ritual of the Temple proceedings and the smoke of the sacrifices constantly rising as the Temple was being built.

Albeit a manifestation of Herod's megalomania, the rebuilding of the Temple complex was timely. The Sanctuary could no longer cope with the

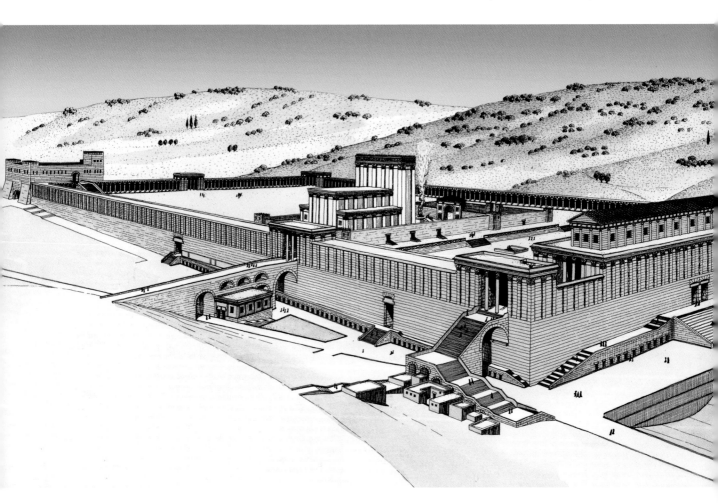

demands of the city's residents, somewhat exaggeratedly estimated by the historian Tacitus as 600,000 (*Histories* 5.13). To this number must be added the multitudes of pilgrims who converged on the city for the three major festivals (Josephus records that during one Passover there were 3 million people in Jerusalem!).

Middot 2.1 describes the Temple as 500 cubits (262.50 m or 861 feet) square. It is now clear that this refers to the original Temple Mount, which was the only part considered holy. Herod doubled its size and although his additions were not considered as part of the sacred enclosure, they must have gone a long way towards alleviating congestion.

The massive undertaking called for a partial cutting away of the high hill located to the north of a fosse which protected the Temple Mount in that direction. The

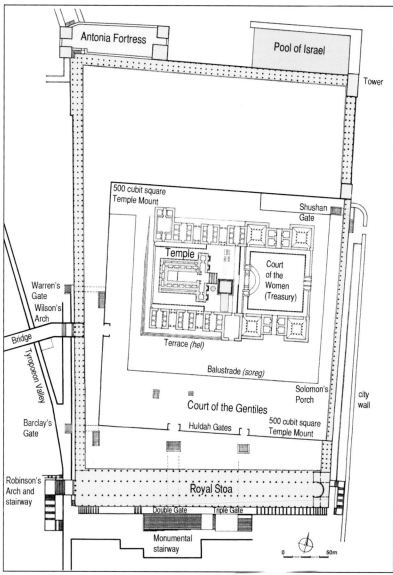

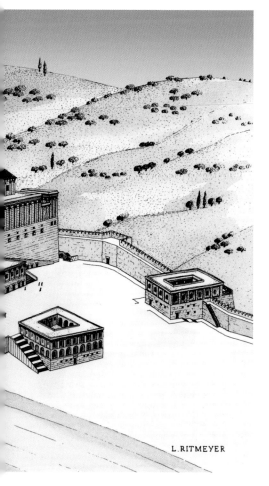

L. RITMEYER

remaining rockscarp provided an almost unassailable foundation for the Antonia Fortress, built at the northwest corner of the newly created Temple Mount.

In the south, the Hasmoneans had already built an extension. Herod extended the platform even farther to the south and then built the magnificent Royal Stoa, which ran the entire length of the new Southern Wall. This wall was pierced by the Double Gate, which was approached by a broad stairway, and the Triple Gate, farther to the east.

The western extension called for a partial filling in of the Tyropoeon Val-

Plan of the Temple Mount during the Second Temple period.

ley. The Western Wall itself had four entranceways: from the north, Warren's Gate, the bridge over Wilson's Arch, Barclay's Gate, and the stairway above Robinson's Arch. These entranceways were all named after explorers of the nineteenth century.

The depth of the Kedron Valley below precluded any possible expansion to the east. The line of the Eastern Wall was therefore merely extended to meet the new north- and southeast corners. Because of its location atop the ancient wall, the eastern portico of the Temple Mount was known as Solomon's Porch. It was here that Jesus was almost stoned one wintry day during the feast of Hanukkah (John 10.22–39), and where the disciples used to congregate and teach following the death of their master (Acts 3.11, 5.12). A low fence (the *Soreg*) marked the separation of the sacred enclosure from the outer Court of the Gentiles and plaques attached at intervals to this fence warned strangers from straying off limits.

Approaching the Temple, each successive area increased in degree of holiness. After the *Soreg* came the Rampart (*Hel*), the terrace that surrounded the Temple on three sides. Next came the Court of the Women, which was as far as women were allowed to proceed, then the Court of the Israelites, the Court of the Priests, the Porch, the Holy and finally the Most Holy, "unapproachable, inviolable, invisible to all" (*War* 5.219). Josephus' description of the exterior of the Temple evinces extraordinary beauty:

> The exterior of the building wanted nothing that could astound either mind or eye. For, being covered on all sides with massive plates of gold, the sun was no sooner up than it radiated so fiery a flash that persons straining to look at it were compelled to avert the eyes, as from solar rays. To approaching strangers it appeared from a distance like a snow-clad mountain; for all that was not overlaid with gold was of purest white.
>
> (*War* 5.222–223)

THE EXCAVATIONS ON THE OPHEL

We begin our circuit of the city, tracing the known elements (see drawing on p. 9), beginning at the southern wall of the Temple Mount. Josephus tells us (*War* 5.145) that the First Wall joined the walls of the Temple Mount at a place called Ophlas (the Ophel). Judging from the size of this building excavated on the Ophel and its close proximity to the Temple Mount, it must have been an important building. Some have identified it as the site of the Akra, the Hellenistic fortress built by Antiochus IV in 186 B.C., to control the Jewish population of the city. As Josephus (*Ant.* 12.362) records:

> At this time the garrison in the Akra of Jerusalem and the Jewish renegades did much harm to the Jews; for when they went up to the temple with the intention of sacrificing, the garrison would sally out and kill them—for the Akra commanded the temple.

Because of the added information given in War 1.39 that it stood "in the lowest portion of the town," it seems logical to look for the Akra in this area. However, because of its low elevation in relation to the Temple, a fortress here would have had to stand 80 m high (an architectural impossibility for that time), to properly guard the Temple Mount.

Rooms, ritual baths and cisterns belonging to a large public building were later constructed inside the ruins of the earlier building. These appear to date from the first century A.D.

During this period, Josephus records a number of palaces being built here in the lower city, namely, the Palace of Queen Helena of Adiabene, a convert to Judaism from Mesopotamia, of her son Monobazus, and of another relative named Grapte. A first-century palace built against the "tower which lieth out," mentioned in the Book of Nehemiah, was excavated, just to the right of the area shown here.

Drawing of a wine cup done in charcoal on one of the vaults. The magnificent shape testifies to the wealth of the inhabitants.

A view of the southern wall of the Herodian Temple Mount and the excavated remains in the Ophel.
In the foreground is a large rockscarp, the result of quarrying in the late Roman period. A series of rooms above the rockscarp, together with those at the bottom left of the picture, belong to a building that probably once extended into the quarried area. In the first, Hellenistic, phase, these rooms were apparently built around a pool. Typical finds of the period include Rhodian-sealed jar handles, indicating a provenance in Rhodes.

A view of the southwest part of the Givati Park excavations. A mikveh with steps descending to the east can be seen at bottom left, next to the ladder. The Herodian vaults are located in the deeper areas in the centre of the picture. At the conclusion of the excavations, a new City of David Centre for visitors, called in Hebrew "Mercaz Kedem" will be built over the archaeological remains found in this area.

The mansion that was excavated in the lower Ophel area, near the modern road, consisted of many rooms, ritual baths (*mikva'ot*), cisterns and cellars. The lower rooms of this large palace-like structure were built into the remains of an earlier building from the First Temple period. In one of these vaulted cellars, a depiction of a wine cup was painted in charcoal on the wall, attesting to the palatial character of this mansion. Four *mikva'ot* are an indication that the inhabitants strictly kept the Jewish laws of purity. Josephus (*War* 6.353–4) wrote that Titus

> gave his troops permission to sack the city. For that day they refrained; but on the next day they set fire to the Archives, the Acra, the council-chamber, and the region called Ophlas (Ophel), the flames spreading as far as the palace of Queen Helena [of Adiabene].

In the excavation, burnt stones were found that testify to the huge conflagration that destroyed this building in 70 A.D. For this reason the mansion has been identified with the Palace of Queen Helena, who, as mentioned, was a convert to Judaism. However, there is no firm evidence to associate it with the residence of the queen.

Here we see one of the many burnt stones that were excavated in one of the mansion's mikvaot. It had a sobering effect on the volunteers that were digging through the Roman destruction debris.

There is another contender for the identification of this famous building farther to the west. In the Givati Parking Lot, down from the Dung Gate and close to the entrance of the City of David archaeological park, the remains of another Herodian building have been excavated. It has very thick walls preserved to a height of 5 m (15 feet) and the basement consists of several vaulted rooms, a regular feature in Herodian buildings. Two *mikva'ot* were found to the immediate north of the basement. In this building, too, the horrors of the Roman destruction are evident. During the siege, the inhabitants cut holes in the walls of the basement in order to escape through the drain underneath the Herodian street that ran alongside its western side. The excavators postulated that the building was purposely destroyed by the Romans, as building stones from the upper rooms were found mixed with the destruction debris in the basement.

It is always attractive to identify the excavated remains with an historical building. The first contender is located on the eastern edge of the Ophel, while the latter is at its very western edge. The two magnificent sites are separated by at least 100 m (330 feet), so it is possible that other buildings existed in between that have not yet been excavated. Until there are other buildings found with which to compare them, neither site can definitely lay claim to that famous palace of Helena, Queen of Adiabene.

THE HASMONEAN TOWER AND THE FIRST WALL

Josephus attributes the construction of the First Wall to the period of the First Temple, writing that "besides the advantage of its position, it was also strongly built, David and Solomon and their successors on the throne having taken pride in the work" (*War* 5.143). Early fortifications in this area were originally discovered by the British and Irish archaeologists, J. G. Duncan and R.A.S. Macalister, who dated their construction to the Jebusite and First Temple periods. During the 1960s, they were again investigated by the British archaeologist Kathleen Kenyon. In the excavations of Yigal Shiloh, between 1978 and 1984, this area was part of "Area G" which became internationally known due to the harassment of the diggers by ultra-Orthodox Jews who feared that tombs in the area were being desecrated.

Shiloh was of the opinion that the city wall in this area had largely been built during the Hasmonean period, with the earlier stepped structure that lay between the two towers used as the basis for a glacis. As these fortifications had weak foundations, the glacis, composed of earth and stones, was designed to help defend against enemy attack. The various styles of masonry found here indicate the First Wall's frequent repairs. Indeed the Book of Maccabees records a number of repairs to the city wall by Hasmonean rulers, e.g., when Jonathan and the elders of the people "gathered together to rebuild the city as part of the wall built over the eastern ravine had fallen" (1 Maccabees 12.37). Although we know that Herod also strengthened the First Wall, it would appear that his repairs were concentrated on the part surrounding the southwestern hill. Only there did the unearthed sections of the First Wall contain ashlars with characteristic Herodian margins.

Below we see one of the projecting towers situated at the crest of the Eastern Hill. This tower was built in the Hasmonean period, while the other earlier remains in this area were covered with a glacis. The various styles of masonry found in sections of the First Wall indicate its frequent repairs during the Hasmonean period.

Reconstruction of the eastern section of the First Wall and its two towers, uncovered in Area G.

At the mouth of the Tyropoeon Valley, a huge stepped water reservoir was excavated. Here we see the steps that allowed people to go down to the water. According to some researchers, this is the Siloam Pool that is mentioned in John ch.9. According to the size, it must have been one of the main water reservoirs in Jerusalem.

The First Wall of the Hasmonean and Herodian periods ran at a higher level along the eastern ridge than did the city wall of earlier periods. However, just to the north of the area shown here, the lines of the earlier and later walls converge and follow the rockscarp that runs to the end of the ridge. Here, the wall incorporated the large dam which crossed the mouth of the Central or Tyropoeon Valley to wind its way around the southwestern hill until it reached Herod's Palace, near the present-day Jaffa Gate.

The dam, composed of a wall some 66 feet (20 m) wide and 300 feet (100 m) long, is strengthened by a series of seven buttresses projecting from the southern face of the wall. The buttresses and underlying wall, together with the southern city gate (at the lower left corner of the drawing), were first discovered in the late 1890s by the British archaeologist F. J. Bliss and architect A. C. Dickie. They used a series of tunnels dug at strategic points to follow the line of the city wall in this area. The archaeological evidence points to a first-century A.D. date for this wall, but it could have been built as early as the Hasmonean period.

The massive wall contained a reservoir that was originally supplied by the Siloam Channel carrying water from the Gihon Spring, Jerusalem's main water source, in a direct line to this pool. This channel should not be confused with Hezekiah's Tunnel, which brought water to the Pool of Siloam located just to the north—the double-gated entranceway to the porticoed building which surrounded it is visible at the top of the drawing.

The rock-hewn Siloam Channel was uncovered for most of its extent, some 1,312 feet (400 m), with apertures through which the cultivated terraces on the eastern ridge could be irrigated. Scholars are generally in agreement that the biblical "waters of Siloam that flow softly" (Isa. 8.6) refer to this channel. To the city's disadvantage, both the channel and the reservoir lay outside the walls of the First Temple period, leaving Jerusalem unprotected and vulnerable.

In 701 B.C., King Hezekiah's conduit, which channelled the waters in an underground tunnel to a new pool inside the city walls, solved the problem in an astute way. This of course meant that the Siloam Channel ceased to be the principal water conduit of the city. However, the recent City of David

The Siloam Pool today.

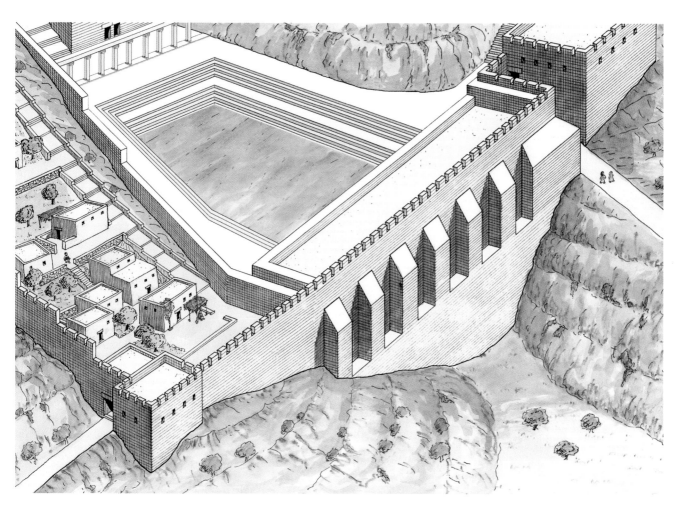

excavations prove that the southern end of the Siloam Channel was integrated into the new scheme and utilized for the overflow of the new Pool of Siloam. This outlet can be seen at the top right. Its location in relation to the new pool caused it to be called the "Lower Pool."

The archaeological evidence shows that reservoirs were built at this spot during various periods. The biblical record in Ecclesiastes (2.5–6) would seem to indicate that we must look to Solomon as the original inventor of this project:

> I made me great works; I builded me houses; I planted me vineyards; I made me gardens and orchards, and I planted trees in them of all kind of fruits; I made me pools of waters, to water therewith the wood that bringeth forth trees.

The obvious insouciance as to any form of protection for the Siloam Channel indicates that it was constructed during a time of peace. Prior to King Hezekiah, only the reign of King Solomon was noted for its tranquillity. Indeed Yigal Shiloh wrote in his excavation report that the Siloam Channel may have served the city in his Stratum 14—tenth century B.C., the very century in which Solomon sat on the throne. Today, the site of the reservoir is known as Birket el-Hamra ("pool of clay soil"), one of the most fertile areas in the city. Fig trees and almond trees grow there in lush abundance.

In the first century A.D., the sight of this area must have contributed to the general impression of a city blessed with a multitude of reservoirs. Historians have often mentioned that despite siege and drought, Jerusalem never experienced a severe water shortage.

Reconstruction of the large dam and reservoir at the southeastern corner of the city.

The Gihon is a typical karstic spring supplied by groundwater that flows down to the hills of Jerusalem from the higher Judean Mountains in the north. Its flow is intermittent and its name Gihon probably derives from the Hebrew *giha*—"gushing forth." The spring could supply up to 1,200 cubic meters per day, depending on the season. Obviously the most advantageous location for collecting these great quantities of water is at the outlet of the Tyropoeon Valley, much like the Siloam Channel that preceded it. Here the water could be efficiently collected, controlled and defended.

From the Gihon Spring, the tunnel followed a serpentine course, probably following a natural fissure in the rock, for 1,750 feet (533 m). The average height of the tunnel is about 7 feet (2 m). To this day the tunnel brings the waters of the Gihon to the Pool of Siloam. The water is now unfit for drinking. During the Second Temple period, many more reservoirs were constructed and many homes had their own cisterns, but the Pool of Siloam was still very much in use and a focal point of the city. Josephus calls it "the fountain of sweet and abundant water" (*War* 5.140).

The Mishnah (*Sukkah* 4.9) records that it was from here that the golden flagon of water for the Water Libation was taken, during the Feast of Tabernacles (Succoth). Para 3.2 records that from here, also, the water for the ashes of the red heifer was collected. The special gushing quality of the waters must have continued to impress the city's populace. In the gospel record of the healing of the blind man (John, ch. 9), Jesus anoints the eyes of the blind man and tells him to "go wash in the Pool of Siloam, which is by interpretation sent."

Shown here is only a small portion of the original Pool of Siloam. This picture was taken from the outlet of Hezekiah's Tunnel and from below the vault that was built following the excavations of Bliss and Dickie in the 1890s to support a mosque above.

King Hezekiah had diverted the waters of the Gihon Spring to the Pool of Siloam by means of an ingenious underground tunnel. As we mentioned earlier, the existing Siloam Channel was adequate only in peacetime, so when King Sennacherib rose up against Jerusalem, King Hezekiah's response was, "Why should the Kings of Assyria come and find much water?" (2 Chron. 32.4).

This reconstruction of the upper Pool of Siloam is based on remains found by the German archaeologist Dr. H. Güthe in 1880 and by Bliss and Dickie in 1896. It is impossible to determine the exact period to which their findings belong, but it would appear that they can be ascribed to the time of King Herod the Great.

According to Bliss and Dickie, the pool also had a double gate similar in function to that of the Temple Mount—one for entering, the other for leaving—as in a mikveh or ritual bath. The plaza and small staircase to the south are also based on archaeological remains.

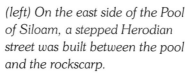

(left) On the east side of the Pool of Siloam, a stepped Herodian street was built between the pool and the rockscarp.

(above) This is the street running alongside the Pool of Siloam and was apparently built in conjunction with the porticoed building that surrounded the pool. It was built in the typical Herodian fashion of "a step and a landing," identical to the stairway leading up to the Double Gate, in the southern wall of the Temple Mount.

Of the two streets, the one on the left is part of the main Tyropoeon street that began in the north, at the Damascus Gate. Beneath this main street ran a drain for rainwater and sewage. The drain has been cleared and can be walked through today. This drain is one of the most important underground passages mentioned by Josephus in which the Jews tried to hide from the Romans in 70 A.D.

The Hinnom Valley today is a dry ravine which separates Mount Zion from the hill of Abu Tor. The valley is known in Arabic as Wadi er-Rababi—the "valley of the lute"—because of its shape. Now landscaped as part of a national park that surrounds the Old City, it is the site of the Greek Orthodox Monastery of St. Onuphrius, in the center of the photograph.

Crusader
charnel
house

"Refuge of
the Apostles"

*Distyle in
antis* tomb

Tomb of
Annas

The walled compound of the Monastery of St. Onuphrius in the Hinnom Valley. Two first-century tombs, one known as the "Refuge of the Apostles" and another with a notable two-pillared porch (known as distyle in antis*), located within the monastery grounds, are part of a lavishly decorated tomb complex. The most outstanding tomb—that of Annas the High Priest—lies outside the walls, on the terrace just below the two slender cypress trees. The ruins of the Crusader vaulted structure are visible near the monastery walls to the center right.*

The southern city gate must have been a scene of startling contrasts. On the one side was an abundance of water, while on the other a path led out of the city into the Judean wilderness. A necropolis, or city of the dead, lay outside the gate, on the rockface of the Hinnom Valley. Its rock-cut tombs were exquisitely decorated in the style of the Second Temple. The most central of these tombs was surmounted by a monument that made it stand out above all the others.

The valley became infamous during the First Temple period due to its sinister biblical associations with child sacrifice to Moloch (Jer. 7.31–32). The idea seems to have been carried over into the New Testament, with its use in the Aramaic form of Gehenna as a metaphor for hell or everlasting punishment (Matt. 10.28). However, the strongest association of this place is with Akeldama, the "field of blood" of the New Testament. This name was given to the Potter's Field, bought by the chief priests for the purpose of burying foreigners with the money the remorseful Judas had flung into the Treasury (Matt. 27.3–9; Acts 1.18–19).

The area was identified as Akeldama as early as the third and fourth centuries by chroniclers such as Eusebius, Jerome and Arculf. In the twelfth century, the Crusaders built a large underground vaulted charnel house to inter the bones of deceased knights and pilgrims.

However, in the first century A.D., this area, far from being a desolate cemetery, was a rather elegant tomb complex decorated in the finest Herodian style. The most splendid tomb, that of Annas the High Priest, will be described more fully in the following pages.

THE TOMB OF ANNAS THE HIGH PRIEST

The tomb of Annas the High Priest. Part of the original triple-gated entrance can still be seen, as can a portion of the scalloped shell design over the central doorway. One of the two apses with benches is visible on the right. They could have served as a resting place for visitors or may have been designed as a post for tomb guards.

The tomb of Annas the High Priest holds a central position in the elaborate tomb complex at the southern end of the Hinnom Valley. Unfortunately, much has been destroyed, but enough has been preserved to suggest that it belonged to a very important personage.

Inside the tomb, the principal chamber has an intact, domed ceiling decorated with an intricate rosette pattern and stylized acanthus leaves at the four corners. Each of the two side walls of this domed tomb chamber had three loculi (*kokhim*) or burial niches. The central kokh of the western wall was once sealed off by the lower half of a false door of the Attic type, that is, one whose side

moldings widen out at the top to give the impression of a lintel. This doorway was not meant to provide passage but was an elaborately decorated burial cavity for a highly honored person—the question is, who?

Josephus, in his record of the siege of Jerusalem by Titus in 70 A.D., describes the final ploy of the Roman leader—the building of a circumvallation or siege wall to block off all escape by the Jews (War 5.504–507). He gives the precise line of the thirty-nine furlong earthworks which were built in three days. From "the hill which overhangs the Siloam ravine," he describes it as inclining westward, then "descending into the Valley of the

Reconstruction of the triple-gated entrance to the anteroom of the tomb of Annas the High Priest. This is based on the remains of the partly preserved scalloped conch above the central doorway and those of four pilasters, the outer ones showing an additional rounded moulding which was part of a frame. The reconstruction of the Triple Gate of the southern wall of Herod's Temple Mount (see page 15) was modeled on the proportions of the triple gate of Annas's tomb. The entrances of these tombs faced north across the valley to the Temple Mount, and were decorated in fine Oriental-Hellenistic style.

Indications of a superstructure, such as that on the tomb of Absalom, suggest that the tomb could be identified as a monument. On the right of the conch decoration, the top of the rock wall is carved in such a way as to receive masonry blocks. By contrast, the nearby tomb known as the "Refuge of the Apostles" had an undecorated band of bedrock above its frieze which would preclude it from ever having had a superstructure.

Fountain," which can be identified as the present-day En-Rogel a little to the south of the foot of the ancient City of David, "beyond which it ascended over against the tomb [Greek: monument] of Ananus the high priest and taking in the mountain where Pompey encamped, turned northwards...." Following the westerly direction indicated by Josephus' description, the siege wall could only have reached the site of Pompey's encampment by ascending the prominent southern rockscarp of the Hinnom Valley where the decorated tomb complex is located.

In contrast to other surrounding tombs, the facade of the triple-gated tomb was continued upward in masonry. This may indicate that it once had a superstructure, which could be seen from afar, making it worthy of mention in Josephus' description of the siege wall. Ananus is to be identified with the High Priest Annas, who held office from 6 to 15 A.D. and who is mentioned a number of times in the New Testament. His five sons all held office for varying periods of time, but it was his son-in-law Caiaphas, who served from 18 to 37 A.D. and presided at the trial of Jesus (Matt. 26.57), who is best known. The tomb of Caiaphas has recently been found in the area of the Jerusalem Forest, some 2 miles (3 km) from this site.

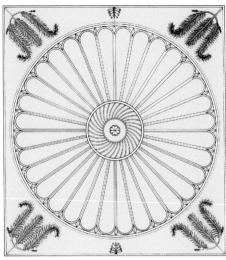

The carved domed ceiling of this tomb distinguishes it from every other Second Temple period tomb in Jerusalem: with one exception, no other tomb contains sculpted internal decoration. Thirty-two petals surround a small whorl rosette at center whose petals are still faintly visible. Stylized acanthus leaves fill the corners.

A reconstructed view of the interior of the tomb chamber. The central tomb in the wall on the right was probably the place where Annas himself was buried.

As for the identification of this cemetery with Akeldama, it seems unlikely that the tombs of impoverished strangers would lie closer to the city than the tomb of the high priestly patriarch and his family. Putting together Josephus' record of the location of the Tomb of Annas and the outstanding decorative style of these tombs, their identification as belonging to this wealthy family appears clearly warranted. The similar decorative style found in architectural elements from near the Temple Mount, as described below, further strengthens this view. It seems appropriate that the other elegantly decorated tombs in the area are grouped around the most elaborate one, the monument of Annas with its scalloped dome.

There is a great resemblance between the carved rosette design in the tomb's main chamber and the rosettes carved onto the domed ceiling in the passageway leading up from the Double Gate. The shape of the Attic doorways inside the tomb is also similar to fragments of Attic doorways found in the Temple Mount excavations.

If the identification of these tombs with those of the family of Annas is correct, it would appear that this priestly family wanted to invest their final resting place with some of the magnificence of the Temple Mount. Especially noteworthy is the resemblance of the entranceway of this tomb to the Triple Gate, through which the priests would enter on their way to the Sanctuary.

THE ESSENE QUARTER

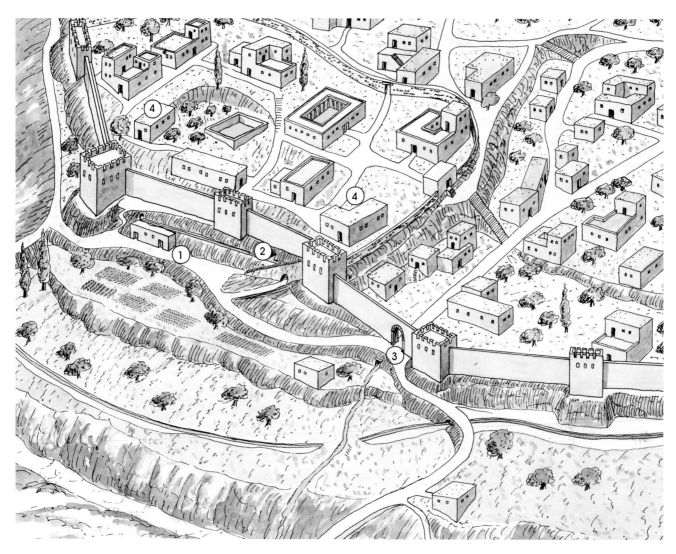

In attempting to trace the line of the First Wall across the southern flank of Mount Zion, we read in Josephus (*War* 5.145) that "it extended through a place called Bethso to the Gate of the Essenes." This cryptic reference has been the cause of much puzzlement to scholars of ancient Jerusalem. What was Bethso and why did the Essenes need their own gate? The Essenes, believed by many to have written the Dead Sea Scrolls found at Qumran, had far stricter rules of purity than those of the Pharisees and Sadducees. Some of them were known

Reconstruction of the Essene Quarter. Bargil Pixner, in his excavations on Mount Zion, was able to identify an ancient outhouse building in this area, the long, low building on the left (1). The name "Bethso" mentioned by Josephus would seem to derive from the Hebrew beth-soa (literally, "house of excrement"). Ritual baths or miqva'ot were also discovered on the rockshelf nearby (2), which would allow the Essenes

to purify themselves after any defilement and reenter the city privately, once the sun had set, through the secret underground gate located just below the ritual baths.

The actual Gate of the Essenes (3) was also discovered by Pixner, as were two large ritual baths (4) just inside the walls. These ritual baths were obviously built to serve the public, and one exceeded in size even the largest mikveh in Qumran.

The Gate of the Essenes was built using the Roman foot (= 11.64 inches), with the outer width of the gate measuring precisely nine Roman feet (105 inches). One of the half-pilasters still preserved at the site has an engraving of Roman letters, marking it as the fourth pilaster supporting the lintel and arch of the gate. In this reconstruction, the actual remains of the gate are colored in darker than the reconstructed masonry.

The Qumran caves, where the Dead Sea Scrolls were discovered.

0   3m

And you shall make them a place for a hand, outside the city, to which they shall go out, to the north-west of the city, (where they shall make) roofed buildings with pits within them, into which the excrement will descend (so that) it will (not) be visible at any distance from the city, three thousand cubits.

(11Q *Miqdash* 46.13–16)

to have lived in Jerusalem. According to the Temple Scroll, the largest of the scrolls, they were to maintain purity in the camp (and they believed Jerusalem to be synonymous with the camp) by preparing a special place:

The Gate of the Essenes discovered by B. Pixner was cut into the old First Wall. A gate in this spot was necessary for the Essenes to access the carefully placed latrines and ritual baths located outside the city wall. The discovery, just inside the walls, of two ritual baths large enough to serve a community and similar to those found at Qumran—combined with all the other hallmarks of an Essene way of life—would seem to indicate that an Essene quarter was located here at the southwest corner of the city during the first century A.D.

THE SERPENT'S POOL

The Serpent's Pool, known today as the Sultan's Pool, was originally built in the Herodian period, and was mentioned by Josephus when recounting the siege of Jerusalem: "and the whole intervening space from Scopus to Herod's monuments, adjoining the spot called the Serpent's Pool, was thus reduced to a dead level" (*War* 5.108). The location of Herod's family tomb in the grounds of the nearby King David Hotel is certain, and this low-lying valley, next to the city, was eminently suitable for a reservoir.

During the Herodian period, fifteen pools were known to have been built in Jerusalem. Their construction at that time was vital to supply the constant need for water by the ever-expanding city. Drinking water was, in the main, supplied by springs and cisterns, but large quantities of water were also required for laundering, industry, construction, and the like.

As a city, Jerusalem is blessed with favorable conditions for excavating pools and collecting water in its surrounding valleys. The Serpent's Pool, one of the few outside the city, was fed by rainwater and by the low-level aqueduct originating from "Solomon's Pools" near Bethlehem. The water was contained by a dam built across the valley, over which a road runs today. Herod had also used the excavated rock in building his nearby palace with its three great towers and the western city wall.

The first-century city apparently had abundant water resources, albeit mostly man-made. Although these pools added a decorative element, they were an absolute necessity. The geographer Strabo described the city thus: "the site is rocky and surrounded by a strong enceinte: within well provided with water, but without absolutely arid" (*Geography* 16.40). The New Testament scene of the wise men leaving the fortified site of Herod's Palace and seeing the star which was to lead them to the stable comes vividly to life as we picture them travelling on their way past the Serpent's Pool to Bethlehem.

The Sultan's Pool, which lies in the shallow bend of the Hinnom Valley at the foot of Mount Zion. The western city wall and the so-called Tower of David are visible at the top right while the houses of Yemin Moshe can be seen opposite, on the left. The now dry pool is used regularly for concerts, hence the podium in the center of the photograph.
The modern name of this pool derives from Sultan Barquq, under whose rule the pool was repaired in 1398. Investigation of the site was carried out by Amos Kloner in 1973.

THE FIRST WALL

The line of the First Wall is traced here, beneath the Ottoman wall just south of the Citadel. The Herodian remains, in the foreground, and the rock foundations, in the center, comprise a revetment wall built against a Hasmonean tower. Further to the right, the Hasmonean First Wall, reinforced by a Herodian outer wall, continues up to the next, also Herodian, tower, built over an earlier Hellenistic one. The first-century Hasmonean wall was largely built of ashlar blocks with drafted margins and coarse protruding bosses. The Herodian outer fortification used the same type of masonry as well as some large, unhewn stones. Josephus, in tracing the First Wall's line around the city, beginning with the Hippicus Tower just north of this area, recounted sixty towers, probably an exaggerated number. The towers shown here were the third and fourth in his reckoning. The First Wall followed the natural contour of the Hinnom Valley, along its steep eastern slope. The thickness of the reinforced walls was designed to support the weight of the raised podium on which Herod's Palace was built on the inside of this wall.

The courtyard of the present-day Citadel, the so-called Tower of David, looking south. The remains we see are a continuation of the First Wall shown in the previous photograph. The city wall curves here to form the northwest corner of the city. On the right of the wall are two projecting towers. The one in the foreground, known as the Middle Tower, was part of the original Hasmonean city fortification that was later reinforced. The modern platform built over it is used for stage performances which take place in the Citadel. In the distance, next to the free-standing arch, the L-shaped wall forms part of another tower. Known as the Southern Tower, it was originally built during the Hasmonean period and contained a mikveh. This massive tower was strengthened and reduced in size during the time of Herod the Great, as part of a general reconstruction of the First Wall. In the left foreground are the sole remains of Herod's Palace.

Of Herod's Palace, Josephus wrote that it baffled all description.

> Indeed, in extravagance and equipment no building surpassed it. It was completely enclosed within a wall thirty cubits high, broken at equal distances by ornamental towers, and contained immense banqueting halls and bedchambers for a hundred guests. The interior fitting are indescribable—the variety of stones (for species rare in every other country were here collected in abundance), ceilings wonderful both for the length of the beams and the splendour of their surface decoration, the host of apartments with their infinite varieties of design, all amply furnished, while most of the objects in each of them were of silver or gold. All around were many circular cloisters, leading one into another, the columns in each being different, and their open courts all of greensward; there were groves of various trees intersected by long walks, which were bordered by deep canals, and ponds everywhere studded with bronze figures, through which the water was discharged, and around the streams were numerous cotes for tame pigeons.
>
> (*War* 5.177–181)

These fountains were probably fed by water which came from the pools in the nearby Hinnom Valley.

Debate as to the location of the Praetorium or Judgment Hall, where Jesus was taken after his condemnation by Pontius Pilate, has long raged among scholars of ancient Jerusalem. The Gospel events make it clear that this building was the residence of Pontius Pilate. After the fall of the Herodian dynasty, Herod's Palace became the residence of the visiting Roman procurators. We know this from a reference in the Roman writer Philo's *Delegation to Gaius* 38, to Pilate's residing in Herod's Palace on the occasion of a Jewish feast. In Josephus' record of the last procurator Cessius Florus, we read of how a raised platform or tribunal was placed in front of the palace, from which he would pronounce judgment (*War* 2.301).

Being Romans, the procurators would have had the same fondness for luxury as did King Herod and would have done their best to maintain the residence with all its sumptuous fittings. Such a backdrop would indeed have been a strange foil for the tragic Gospel scene.

The Hippicus Tower

Since the Byzantine period, the Citadel has been traditionally known as the Tower of David. However, the structure is, apart from the narrower upper portion, completely Herodian. During the recent excavations led by Hillel Geva, it has been identified as the Tower of Hippicus, one of the three great fortified towers built by Herod the Great to protect his palace. Hippicus was the name of his friend who had fallen in battle. Herod named the other two towers after Phasael, his brother, and Mariamme, his wife, whom he had murdered. The respective heights of these towers were 80 cubits (138 feet or 42 m), 90 cubits (155 feet or 47 m) and 55 cubits (95 feet or 29 m). Their height and the lofty site on which they stood added to the impression of impregnable fortifications. Thus Herod commanded access to the city from faraway Jaffa, Gaza and Hebron.

Apart from the remains of the Temple Mount, the Hippicus Tower is the best preserved remnant of the Herodian period in Jerusalem. We owe its rare state of preservation to the awe with which Titus viewed these towers after his capture of the city. "God indeed," he exclaimed, "has been with us in the war. God it was who brought down the Jews from these strongholds; for what power have human hands or engines against these towers?" (*War* 6.411). When he ordered all the rest of the city to be razed, he left only these three towers and

the portion of the wall enclosing the

The entrance to the Citadel, 19th century engraving.

Looking from within the courtyard of the Citadel in a northeasterly direction—opposite to the previous photograph—we again see the First Wall. The wall abuts a large tower with a row of flags. Although traditionally known as the Tower of David, it dates almost entirely to the Herodian period, and has been identified with the Tower of Hippicus.

Remains of the other two towers have not yet been found, probably because, in contrast to the Hippicus Tower, they were not incorporated in the western line of the city wall in later periods.

city on the west: the latter as an encampment for the garrison that was to remain, and the towers to indicate to posterity the nature of the city and of the strong defenses which had yet yielded to Roman prowess.

(*War* 7.2)

In the foreground of the drawing

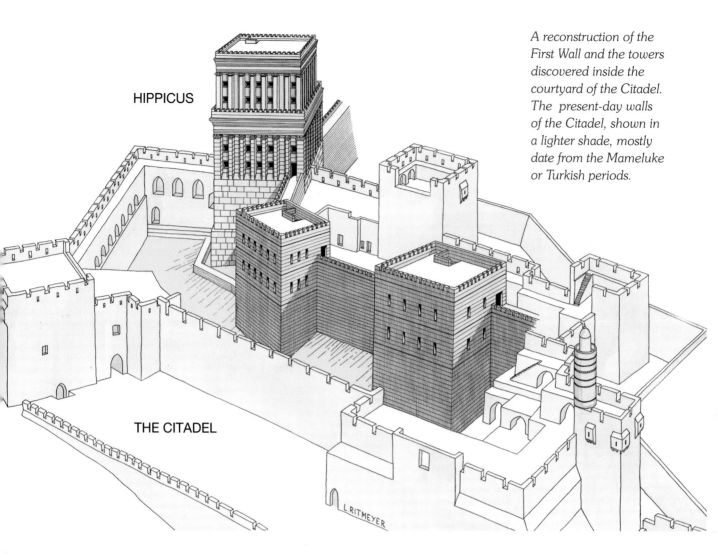

HIPPICUS

THE CITADEL

L RITMEYER

A reconstruction of the First Wall and the towers discovered inside the courtyard of the Citadel. The present-day walls of the Citadel, shown in a lighter shade, mostly date from the Mameluke or Turkish periods.

are the original Hasmonean Southern and Middle Towers which Herod had strengthened. The Hippicus Tower stands at the northwest corner of the First Wall. Titus had admired all three towers' "solid, lofty mass" (*War* 6.410). In the late nineteenth century, the German architect Conrad Schick investigated the Hippicus Tower and confirmed that its structure was indeed solid.

Although the other two towers were originally Hasmonean and later strengthened by Herod, the three great towers of Hippicus, Phasael and Mariamme were entirely new con-structions incorporated into the Hasmonean First Wall. The Hippicus Tower is founded on bedrock and stands today at a height of 62 feet (19 m). Each stone course is set back slightly from the preceding one. Josephus informs us that "above this solid and compact mass of masonry was a reservoir, twenty cubits deep, to receive the rainwater, and over this a double-roofed chamber, twenty-five cubits high, with roofs of diverse colours" (*War* 5.164–165). However, these were located in the upper part of the tower that was destroyed. As evidenced by Herod's desert refuges, such as Herodium, Masada, Cypros and Hyrcania, we see how desperately the paranoid king craved the security such a fortification with ample water supplies can give.

The Northern Palace at Masada, one of Herod's refuges.

Soon after the Six-Day War in 1967, extensive excavations, headed by Nahman Avigad, were carried out in the Jewish Quarter of Jerusalem's Old City. The pavement shown here, which was found in Area J of the excavations, was identified by Avigad as part of a street built in the late Herodian period, when the Temple Mount project had already been completed, resulting in massive unemployment. In order to provide work, the streets of Jerusalem were paved in white stone (Ant. 20.219– 222).

The pavement extended for about 164 feet (50 m). The paving slabs were unusually large in size. The largest measured approximately 8 feet (2.5 m) long and some 20 inches (50 cm) thick. They were obviously designed as foundation stones for a large paved area, with the surviving remains pointing to a width of at least 50 feet (15 m). Because of its location and unusually large width, the author has proposed a different identification for the paved area to the one suggested by Avigad.

Area J is located on the easternmost of the two prominent peaks of the former Upper City of Jerusalem. Herod's Palace was constructed on the more westerly peak, occupying a prime defensive position. From Josephus' record of the reign of Agrippa, we learn that the old Hasmonean Palace had also stood in a prominent position:

> being situated on a lofty site, [it] afforded a most delightful view to any who chose to survey the city from it. The King was enamoured of this view and used to gaze, as he reclined at meals there, on everything that went on in the Temple.
>
> *(Ant. 20.190)*

No trace of the Hasmonean Palace itself has yet been found. However, one may assume that Herod's successors would have attempted to embellish the old palace, which had to suffice for the one built by their infamous predecessor and abruptly taken from them. Agrippa's huge chamber, from which the Temple proceedings could be viewed, was one innovation. In a similar vein, a new plaza of large paving stones would have afforded a grander entrance to the palace and made it stand out from the surrounding buildings. This construction could well have been part of the massive project of paving the streets of Jerusalem that was undertaken at the end of the Second Temple period.

This pavement, today in the Hurvah Square, was removed from its original location, some 20 to 30 feet (10–15 m) to the northeast, because of rebuilding in the area.

THE GENNATH (GARDEN) GATE

The wall here formed part of a complex of walls found in an area with limited access for digging. To the south of this eastern section, at a distance of 16 feet (5 m), there is another parallel wall-fragment. If the people in the illustration were to look to their right, they could see the remains of a passageway formed by the two walls.

This site lies along the assumed line of the old First Wall. From the Tower of Mariamme, the wall ran in an easterly direction until it reached the western wall of the Temple Mount. Josephus recounts that the Second Wall began at "the gate in the First Wall which they called Gennath and enclosing only the northern district of the town went up as far as Antonia" (*War* 5.146). Prior to the Jewish Quarter excavations, the exact position of the Gennath Gate could not be determined. All that was known was that it was located in the northern part of the First Wall and that there were gardens in the vicinity, hence the name Gennath, derived from the Hebrew for garden. However, the location of Golgotha, which was outside the city walls and which the gospels relate was near a garden, depended on its position.

The wall remains found in the northern part of the Jewish Quarter definitely point to a gate-like construction. It would appear that the entrance to the city here was through the passageway visible in the photo. The wall section to the left (west) of the seam was the beginning of another tower and/or wall running north from this gate. An identification of these remains as the Gennath Gate accords with Josephus' account that the Second Wall began at the Gennath Gate. The fact that the main city gate from the late First Temple period was located just to the east of this gate lends weight to

The remains of a wall, 15 feet (4.60 m) thick, were found in the Jewish Quarter excavations between Habad Street and Jewish Quarter Street. Pottery finds indicate that the wall dates from about the second century B.C. Its crucial feature is the vertical line at which the two men in the photograph are looking. This "seam" divides the wall into two sections: the distant one is of superior quality masonry to the one in the foreground (on the east).
The column base on the top right of the wall is from the Byzantine street known as the Cardo, which was later built over these remains.

this identification. The location of both fortified gateways was dictated by the same topographical considerations, i.e., to defend the city wall along the Transversal Valley, a weak spot in the city's defenses.

During the Herodian period, the Upper City was the residential area favored by the wealthy nobility. The houses were densely built compared with the earlier Hasmonean period, when there was much more space between the houses. However, their lavish interior decoration gave them the appearance of villas of the utmost luxury. Spacious in plan, these residences were decorated according to the high standards of the day, as evidenced by walls with frescoes and stucco, as well as the remains of ten decorated mosaic floors.

The mosaic seen here is one of the largest and finest found in these excavations. It belonged to the living room of dwelling unit D in the middle block of the now preserved Herodian Quarter. The central motif differs from the more usual rosette design and is comprised of interlacing meanders which form swastika patterns. The frame is composed of triangular, guilloche, and wave-crest patterns. As we see, the mosaic, although not found in its complete state, was probably square in design, as was usual for the mosaics found in these Herodian villas. The missing parts of the mosaic floor were restored by layers of plaster up to floor level, with the outline of the original pattern then traced in the plaster.

The restored room exhibits furniture in a setting typical of the period. Food would have been served from the high stone table, to guests reclining on couches and eating from low round tables with wooden legs. The Jewish inhabitants of such residences would have used large lathe-turned stone vessels, such as we see here, for they were not subject to ritual impurity as were clay vessels.

Judging by their size and sophisticated architectural style, the fragments displayed here probably belonged to public buildings of large dimensions. However, since such fragments were usually found in excavation rubble or in secondary use in buildings from a later period and not in situ, it is difficult to ascribe them to a particular building.

From left, the first element is a fragment of a Doric cornice with a proposed reconstruction on the panel behind it. The second element, with the triglyph, also formed part of a large Doric frieze, an architectural component only used in important monumental buildings. The two volutes belonged to massive Ionic capitals of the same type as a complete example, which is not exhibited here in the Herodian Quarter but set up out-of-doors in the nearby Batei Mahsse courtyard. (This Ionic capital has been adopted by R.A.D. as its logo!) A drawing showing the original height of an Ionic column crowned by such a capital is displayed on the right-hand panel.

The Corinthian capital in the center of the photograph is a replica, the original on exhibit in the United States. This capital was found in an unusually fine state of preservation in a level that could be clearly dated by coins to the First Revolt, prior to the destruction of the city in 70 A.D. The small Doric capital was included in order to complete the representation of the three architectural orders—Corinthian, Ionic and Doric.

These remains clearly indicate that, in the Jerusalem of the Herodian period, the art of decorative architectural stone-carving had reached a level that could be compared with the great temple sanctuaries of the day, such as Baalbek (in Lebanon) and Palmyra (in Syria).

Architectural elements from the Herodian villas found in the Jewish Quarter excavations.

Seven-branched menorah (lampstand), with indications of the altar of incense, the table of shewbread, and steps for the menorah, incised in plaster, from Herodian period, found in the Jewish Quarter excavations.

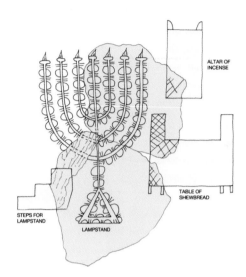

The so-called Palatial Mansion was located on the eastern slope of the Upper City just opposite the southwest corner of the Temple Mount. Built on two levels, the ground floor was designed as living quarters while the lower level contained storerooms and water installations.

Its overall plan, centered around a paved courtyard, is evidence that, despite its large size, it was a single unit and not divided into smaller residences. The entrance to the building (1) was from the west via steps leading down into a vestibule (2), where a mosaic floor with a central rosette pattern was found almost completely intact, with the charred beams of the ceiling lying on top of it.

From the vestibule, one could either turn into the fresco room (3) on the right, which had panels painted in red and yellow on its plastered walls in the style of the Pompeian frescoes or, to the left, into the magnificent Reception Room (4) with its stuccoed walls and ceiling.

From the vestibule, the visitor entered directly into the courtyard (5), to reach the rooms of the eastern wing. Of this wing only one of the ground-floor rooms, a bathroom (6), with a low bench

and a stepped sitting pool, has been preserved. Its floor was paved with a simple patterned mosaic. This bathroom was probably used before descending into one of the two mikvehs that lay underneath the courtyard and which are not visible here.

A stairway on the northern side of the courtyard leads down to the basement

level of the eastern wing. Again there is a vestibule (7) from which one could gain access to a large vaulted storeroom (8) on the west. On the basement's eastern side were two additional mikvehs, one of which had a side bath (9). The second mikveh (10), in the foreground of the drawing, was much larger and had a vaulted ceiling. This mikveh was exceptional in that it had a double doorway and an entrance porch paved with mosaics.

The sumptuous fittings of this major structure make it worthy of the term "palace." It contains four ritual baths, one of which, with its separate doors for entry and exit, evidently served a number of people. This, coupled with the traces found of a great conflagration, point to a possible identification with the palace of Annas the High Priest. The high priest's palace is recorded by Josephus (*War* 2.426) as having been burnt together with the palace of Agrippa and Berenice in 70 A.D. It was only a short walk from here to the Royal Bridge, where the priests could cross directly to the Temple platform without first having to descend into the Tyropoeon Valley.

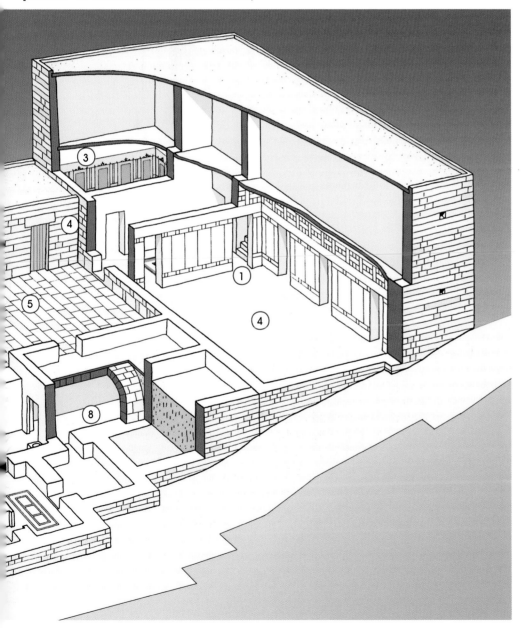

Reconstruction of the Herodian mansion. The excavations in the Jewish Quarter uncovered this residence dating from the Second Temple period. Known as the Palatial Mansion because of its unusually large size—6,500 sq. feet (600 sq.m)—it is now part of the restored Herodian Quarter.

The reconstruction drawing of the Reception Room (p. 46) gives an idea of what an elegant room this once was. This room, which would better be described as a hall, measures 33 by 21 feet (11 by 6.50 m). Because of its large size, it is assumed that it was used to receive guests and for various functions. As mentioned earlier, the mansion, of which the Reception Room is a part, may be identified with the palace of Annas the High Priest.

The Gospel record speaks of Jesus being interrogated by the priests, elders and council in the palace of the High Priest, who at that time was Caiaphas, son-in-law of Annas (Matt. 26.57; Mark 14.53 and Luke 22.54). However, John's Gospel 18.13 intimates that the director of the first interrogation was Annas himself. The task of harmonizing this gospel record with those of the Synoptic gospels would be far less difficult if we were to assume that the old High Priest's Palace of Annas continued to be used for such functions, even if it was a relative of his and not he himself that held the office. He was, after all, as we have seen earlier, a type of *éminence grise* who continued to direct affairs by promoting members of his own family to the high priest's office, long after he himself had vacated it.

It must be said that the plan of this Palatial Mansion, with its central courtyard and lavish reception hall, makes possible a visualization of the scene of Peter warming himself near an outdoor fire while Jesus is interrogated within. Just to the north, however (in the foreground of the drawing), across a narrow alleyway, lie the fragmented remains of a building which clearly had a peristyle, that is, a courtyard surrounded by a colonnade, the single such find from Herodian Jerusalem. This is obviously another potential site of the High Priestly palace.

A certain identification is impossible, as only parts of the Upper City in the present-day Jewish Quarter of the Old City have been excavated. However, the architectural details of the Palatial Mansion and its location allow for the imaginative exercise of painting a backdrop to the dramatic Gospel account.

The Stucco Walls

The walls of this magnificent room were apparently decorated with white stucco, large portions of which were found still adhering to them. The northern wall was in the best state of preservation, with the stucco remains preserved almost to the height of the ceiling.

The basic decorative pattern was well represented on the remaining walls. It consisted of broad panels in between two

A view of the stucco fragments found in the northern wall of the Reception Room. The author, who was in charge of the restoration project, is near the top of this wall. Having worked out the pattern on paper and built up the wall to the original height, he traces the pattern on plaster for proper restoration. The fragment found in the debris has been integrated into the final restoration of the room.

bands of imitation masonry, modeled on "headers and stretchers." However, on the basis of the stucco remains of the northern wall that extended to the greatest height, it was clear that there was an additional band of decoration just below the ceiling. This different style of imitation stone work could only be reconstructed on the basis of a complete panel which was found in the debris on the floor below this wall.

The photograph below shows the northern wall after restoration work had been completed. Standing on scaffolding next to the wall is David Shimon, a master plasterer who learned the skill of working in stucco (plaster work in relief) in his native Iran, prior to his immigration to Israel. In accordance with conservation guidelines, it was decided to distinguish between old and new plaster by using a slightly lighter color for the restored parts of the stucco. Thus, in this view, the original stucco is darker and is visible in the lower part of the illustration, on either side of the scaffolding.

The original process of stucco decoration was studied in adjacent rooms of the Palatial Mansion, which were undergoing a redecoration process from fresco to stucco just before the destruction of this complex in 70 A.D. It was learned that after the stones had been plastered over, the design was pencilled on. Over these pencil lines, a roughly 4 inch (10 cm) wide band of fine white plaster was applied, into which a groove was cut where the original pencil line had been drawn. Wooden strips were placed centrally over the grooves, creating shallow geometrical areas which were filled with plaster. When the plaster was dry, the wooden strips were removed and the pattern would then stand out in relief. This original technique was followed during the restoration of the stucco walls.

The Ceiling

In the excavations, the floor was found littered with small fragments of decorated stucco with different patterns, which had fallen from the ceiling. Before restoration work on the Palatial Mansion began, Nahman Avigad, the project director, gave the author three large trays of a representative sample of ceiling fragments and asked him to try and make some

(overleaf)
Reconstruction of the Reception Room in the Palatial Mansion, based strictly on the excavated fragments and, where necessary, on parallels from contemporary architecture. The pattern on each of the walls, especially the northern wall (in the back), was carefully studied before drawing the walls to their full height. In the western wall (on the left) are three openings which led into small side-rooms. Windows were probably built into the eastern wall (right), which faces the courtyard, in order to provide light. This is corroborated by the finds nearby of building blocks which appear to have been used in some type of window construction.
The exact ceiling height is unknown. Therefore, in the restored room in the Herodian Quarter, a wooden ceiling, part of which has the original geometrical designs reconstructed in plywood and glued onto it, is suspended over the walls to indicate the element of uncertainty.

The northern wall after restoration work.

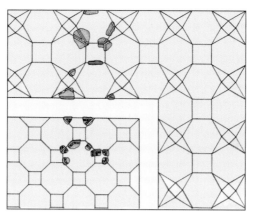

Reconstruction of the pattern used in the ceiling of the Reception Room in the Palatial Mansion, based on excavated fragments.

sense of them. All the pieces showed geometrical patterns in relief—raised sections separated by a narrow band with a groove cut in its center, picked out in red paint. It was clear that the original design must have been divided into two parts, as some fragments had an "egg-and-dart" motif—a pattern based on alternate eggs and arrow-heads, while the remainder were plain.

Measuring the angles in the first group, squares, octagons and triangles of 45 degrees could be discerned. The second group consisted of squares, hexagons and triangles of 30 degrees. After trying out various possibilities and taking into consideration the dimensions of the room, the number of fragments found and their representative proportions, the author came up with the design above.

Accordingly, a band, just over 3.5 feet (1 m) in width, of hexagonal patterns surrounded the ceiling of the room, while the central panel was divided into two squares of a design based on octagons, with a narrow strip in between. The octagonal pattern was formed using the fragments with the "egg-and-dart" motif, while the hexagonal pattern, which had as its basis four hexagons attached to the four sides of a square, used the plain fragments. This design is conjectural but fits in well with the room and has definite parallels with patterns preserved in the vaulted stucco ceilings at Pompeii dating from the first century B.C., as well as in the stone ceilings of the ancient temples of Baalbek and Palmyra.

Judaea Capta coin minted in Rome in honor of the Roman victory over Judaea. Obverse: bust of the Emperor Vespasian. Reverse: a Jewess seated, mourning, beside a plundered statue, with "Judaea" in Latin inscribed below.

The so-called Burnt House was one of many in the Upper City set ablaze by the Romans once victory was theirs in 70 A.D. Josephus (*War* 6.403–407) describes the final torching of the quarter, which fell one month after the Temple was taken:

> Pouring into the alleys, sword in hand, they massacred indiscriminately all whom they met, and burnt the houses with all who had taken refuge within. Often in the course of their raids, on entering the houses for loot, they would find whole families dead and the rooms filled with the victims of the famine, and then, shuddering at the sight, retire empty-handed. Yet, while they pitied those who had thus perished, they had no similar feelings for the living, but, running everyone through who fell in their way, they choked the alleys with corpses and deluged the whole city with blood, insomuch that many of the fires were extinguished by the gory stream. Towards evening they ceased slaughtering, but when night fell the fire gained the mastery, and the dawn of the eighth day of the month Gorpiaeus broke upon Jerusalem in flames.

Heartrending testimony to the accuracy of his record was found in the kitchen of this house—the skeletal arm and hand of a young woman, who had attempted to flee when she realized what was happening but was engulfed in the flames. Apart from the kitchen, the complex consisted of a small courtyard, four rooms and a mikveh.

It would appear from the nature of the complex and from the many ovens found there that it was used as a type of workshop located well out of sight under

Stone weight from the Burnt House inscribed "(belonging) to the son of Kathros."

a large building. A stone weight inscribed with the words "[of] Kathros" points to a connection with another of the high priestly families, the House of Kathros, infamous for their cruel way with the written word, "Woe is me because of the House of Kathros, woe is me because of their pens" (from a satirical song preserved in the Babylonian Talmud, *Pesahim* 57.1). The workshop may have been used in the manufacture of spices for the incense or anointing oil used in the daily Temple service. If so, this would indeed have been a profitable industry and one which this family may well have appropriated to itself.

However, our particular interest for the present purpose is Jerusalem in 30 A.D., so let us try to imagine life in the quarter at that time. Whenever residents and visitors alike would pass these modern residences, they would have been forcibly reminded of the illegitimacy of their high priesthood. Since the beginning of Herod's reign in 37 B.C., only one (the first) of their high priests had come from a legitimate Zadokite family. The others came from either the family of Boethus (of which the House of Kathros was an offshoot), Annas or Phiabi, low-born families which once they had risen to power strove to keep the office for as long as possible.

Found in 1970, early on in the excavations when the rebuilding of the Jewish Quarter was gathering momentum, the Burnt House became a national symbol. It evoked the drama of the nation's history from tragic destruction, through two thousand years of dispersion to triumphant rebirth.

One of the larger rooms found in the basement of the Burnt House, in the Jewish Quarter excavations. Vessels, pieces of collapsed furniture and charred wooden beams were left where they fell. The room's stone walls have not been cleaned or restored and the original soot from the fire is still visible. It is an image frozen in time. Underneath this room lay a vaulted structure that needed to be excavated for a complete archaeological record. With this done, the scene of destruction was painstakingly recreated.

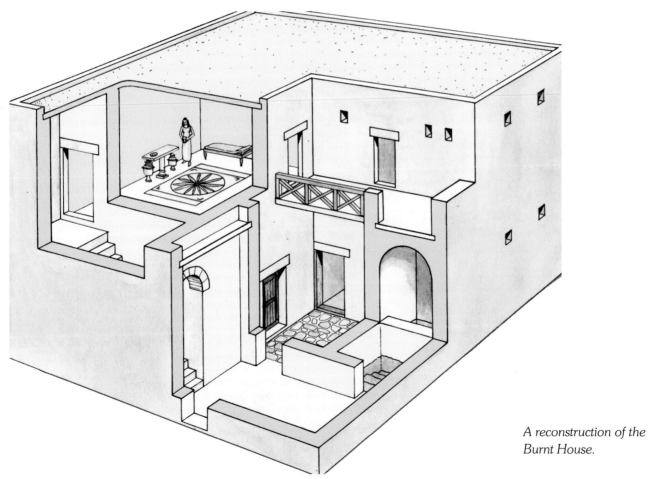

A reconstruction of the Burnt House.

Coin of Agrippa I. According to Josephus, this king attempted to dissuade the Jews, assembled in the Xystus, from going to war with Rome.

When Josephus described the First Wall as it ran eastward from Hippicus Tower, he writes that "it extended to the Xystus, and then joining the council-chamber terminated at the western portico of the temple" (*War* 5.144). From *War* 6.354 we get the additional information that the Archives building, where the city records were kept, was located in the area near the Council Chamber.

Scholars are of the opinion that the Xystus was a place of mass assembly, located on the site of the former Hellenistic Gymnasium originally built by Jason. This Gymnasium and the attendant Hellenistic atmosphere had such an influence that

> the priests ceased to show any interest in the services of the altar; scorning the temple, neglecting sacrifices, they would hurry to take part in the unlawful exercises on the training ground as soon as the signal was given for the discus.
>
> (2 Maccabees 4.9–15)

It has been suggested that it was in the former Gymnasium that Peter addressed the multitude of converts after the descent of the Holy Spirit at Pentecost (Acts 2.1–41). The purpose of the Council Chamber is unclear apart from the fact that it must have served some public function.

Interior view of the Masonic Hall, as it appears today.

If we combine the results of excavations carried out in the nineteenth century and modern-day excavation projects with information contained in the ancient sources, we can pinpoint the location of these buildings with considerable accuracy. The fact that the area has been cleared to create a plaza makes it even easier to visualize. We know the line of the Western Wall and the line of the Royal Bridge, crossing Wilson's Arch. The existence of another arch just to the west can also be proven—steps preserved above this arch have recently been uncovered near the Gate of the Chain. The Masonic Hall, first discovered by Charles Warren in 1868, is oriented northwest, not parallel to the Western Wall, and has been identified as belonging to the Council Chamber.

The existence of a street running alongside the Council Chamber in the direction of Damascus Gate can be inferred from remains found in the Temple Mount excavations. Here, a Herodian paved street which skirted the Western Wall, but also showed evidence of a branch that veered off in a north-westerly direction, was uncovered. The line of a Herodian drain in the excavations can be traced way below the proposed line of this street, in the Tyropoeon Valley bed, beneath the Western Wall plaza.

The building of the Xystus would have required a large flat area and so must have occupied the lower slopes of the Western Hill and part of the valley on the western side of the street just described. There is a vivid scene painted by Josephus in *War* 2.344 where King Agrippa delivers an emotional speech to the Jews assembled in the Xystus in an attempt to dissuade them from war with the Romans. One detail given by Josephus is that Agrippa placed his sister Berenice in a commanding position on the roof of the Hasmonean Palace, "which stood above the Xystus on the opposite side of the upper town," leaving no doubt as to the location of the palace in relation to the Xystus. It is probable then that the Archives building stood on the slope between the palace and the Xystus.

L. RITMEYER

The Masonic Hall, which, as we mentioned, has been identified as the Council Chamber, remains essentially a mysterious building. Charles Wilson, who collaborated with Warren, wrote:

> the object and age of the "Masonic Hall" are most puzzling questions; the low level at which the chamber lies shows that it must have been built long before any such scheme as that of Wilson's Arch forms part was thought of, and its position seems to indicate that it was in some way connected with the Temple, possibly a guardhouse erected during the stormy period of the Maccabees.
>
> ("The Masonry of the Haram Wall," *PEF Quarterly Statement*, 1880, 28)

The name "Masonic Hall" was ascribed by Warren because of an association with Freemasons at the time of its discovery.

Today, more than a century later, little more insight into its original significance has been gained, although its identification as the Council Chamber

mentioned by Josephus has gained wide acceptance. We may surmise that this building was a type of municipal office from where the day-to-day business of the city was supervised.

The interior measurements of the hall are 23×33 feet (7×10 m) and its original walls were over 3 feet (1 m) thick. The inner walls are built of plain dressed stone with an almost perfectly smooth finish, without the use of mortar. On the exterior, the stones have margins and bosses, identical to the Herodian masonry of the Temple Mount walls. It had a double-gated entrance, similar to that of the Double Gate in the southern wall of the Temple Mount. Two pilasters flanked this gateway on the inside and remains of others were preserved above the cyma reversa moulding which projects from the wall. These pilasters were crowned with Corinthian capitals, but only one interior corner capital has survived. The present-day vaulted ceiling is thought to have been constructed in a later period.

A reconstruction of the Masonic Hall, or Council Chamber. The remains show that this was part of a complex system of vaults, lying west of Wilson's Arch beneath the present-day Street of the Chain. On the left, a corner construction is visible suggesting that it was originally part of a larger building. Whatever its original function, this hall is an outstandingly beautiful structure of the period. It reminds us again of the standards of architectural excellence that were then achieved.

THE WESTERN WALL PLAZA—SITE OF
THE XYSTUS AND COUNCIL CHAMBER

The present-day Western Wall Plaza is considered the site of the Xystus and Council Chamber in King Herod's time. Facing the Western Wall, the modern plaza was created to accommodate pilgrims and visitors and to provide space for the ceremonies that regularly take place here. This site is now the nation's focal point, corresponding to the area of important public buildings described by Josephus as located at the termination point of the First Wall by the Western Wall of the Temple Mount.

Let us now locate these elements in the photograph. Access to Wilson's Arch, the last arch of the causeway known as the Royal Bridge, is via the small arch in the building below the minaret. The Masonic Hall, or Council Chamber, is located behind the long low modern building in the center. From what we have said, the location of the Xystus can only have been located between the small arch to the left of the long low building and the buildings farthest left. The proposed location of the Archives building is to the left, outside the picture.

The Pool of Bethesda, or Birket Israil, as it was called in this 19th century engraving.

A Roman relief discovered in the vicinity of the Bethesda, or Sheep Pools, apparently connected with the worship of Serapis, the god of healing.

The remains of the Pools of Bethesda are located near the present-day St. Stephen's or Lions' Gate of the Old City. The pools were first excavated at the end of the nineteenth century by the architect C. Mauss, who had the task of restoring the adjoining Crusader Church of St. Anne, and by the White Fathers, to whom the site belongs. The site was much expanded in the 1956 excavation of J. Roussée of the city's Dominican École Biblique. Interest in the Bethesda Pools stems from the reference to them in John 5.2: "Now there is at Jerusalem by the Probatica a pool, which is called in the Hebrew tongue Bethesda, having five porches." (Probatica in Greek means simply "of sheep" and has been variously translated as sheep market, sheep gate or sheep pool.)

Père L. H. Vincent, the French Dominican archaeologist, puts forward the case for a translation of Probatica as "sheep pool" where the sheep destined for sacrifice were washed. The Book of Nehemiah, in connection with the rebuilding of the city walls, also refers to a Sheep Gate in the northern wall of the Temple Mount. This would indicate that the northern gate of Herod's expanded Temple Mount retained the name Sheep Gate, as it can only have been through this gate that the sacrificial animals were brought into the Temple Mount.

The pools are located about 260 feet (80 m) outside this northern gate, in accordance with the description given in the gospel record. The name Bethesda can be translated "House of Mercy" and may correspond to a similar name mentioned in the Copper Scroll found at Qumran, as the location of hidden treasure.

The remains unearthed at the site point to a complex history with many modifications and additions during the various periods. In the first stage of its development, during the First Temple period, there was only one pool, corresponding to the northernmost of today's twin pools. This pool was formed by building a dam across the Beth Zetha Valley to collect the stream waters which flowed through the valley. An elaborate sluice system allowed this water to be channelled to the northern part of the City of David.

During the Second Temple period, an additional pool was built to the south, on the other side of the original dam. It is unclear when exactly the second pool was built, in the Hellenistic, Hasmonean or Herodian period. Some scholars identify this second pool as the one referred to in Ecclesiastes 50.3 as built by Simon the Hasmonean High Priest for the purpose of supplying water to the Temple. However, pools were usually dug to provide building material as well as to supply water. It therefore seems more likely that Simon would have excavated his pool on the Temple Mount in order to facilitate the Hasmonean extension of the Temple Mount southwards.

A church was built on the site during the Byzantine period which had its western end projecting into the pools, while the eastern half stood on firm ground. The nave of this basilica was built on the dam which separated the two pools. Two massive series of arches, sunk into the pools on either side of the dam, supported the two side aisles. During the Crusader period a small church (or moustier) was built over the ruins of the earlier one. By this time, the pools had been almost completely filled in and pilgrims wishing to visit had to descend by means of a staircase built into the northern basin.

No trace of the five porches mentioned in John's Gospel and confirmed by many chroniclers of the Byzantine period has yet been found. However, an indication of how they may have functioned is given by Origen (231) and Cyril (347), both of whom record that there were four porticoes around the sides and one in the middle. It is a logical solution and, as no better one has been put forward, has received general acceptance. However, one wonders how the sick could have

A reconstruction of the Pools of Bethesda. The plan of the Pools of Bethesda in the first century A.D. is well known from the excavations. Each pool measured approximately 312 by 164–196 feet (95 by 50–60 m) and almost 50 feet (15 m) deep. The pools were cut into the living rock, a task facilitated by their location in the bed of the Beth Zetha Valley.

ventured into either of these pools because of their great depth. So, where was the water the paralytic man sought so desperately to receive healing?

East of the twin pools, five natural caves were discovered, each plastered with steps and a basin for bathing. Nearby was a small temple-like building with a mosaic floor and frescoed walls. From the many small votive offerings found at the site, it is clear that a cult dedicated to the god of healing, Serapis, was practiced here. The excavators believe that this pagan healing center dates back to the Hellenistic period, although the temple was not actually constructed until Roman times. During the Second Temple period, it may have been under Jewish control, although officially with displeasure.

It has been suggested that the sick, after waiting in the shelter of the porticoes that surrounded the two large pools, hoped to be carried into one of the smaller pools when "an angel went down at a certain season into the pool, and troubled the water: whosoever then first after the troubling of the water stepped in was made whole of whatsoever disease he had" (John 5.4). This theory, although reconciling in part the archaeological remains with the gospel record, cannot be proven. However, it is certain that somewhere here, in the vicinity of the Beth Zetha Valley, where the topography is conducive to the building of pools, Jesus healed the man who had been paralyzed for thirty-eight years.

GOLGOTHA—ALTERNATIVE SITES

The Church of the Holy Sepulchre

The Church of the Holy Sepulchre is one of the two main claimants for the site of Jesus' crucifixion, burial and resurrection. The church is located in the Christian Quarter of today's Old City. The Church of the Holy Sepulchre is Christendom's main shrine and probably its most confusing. It consists of a chaotic jumble of assorted remains from various periods, chiefly Byzantine and Crusader, with some repairs carried out in the nineteenth century. The facade shown here is completely Crusader. The twin portals are adorned with pointed arches over which runs a moulding of acanthus and medallions. The door on the right was blocked up by the Muslims sometime after the fall of Crusader Jerusalem in 1187, so that access to the church could be more strictly controlled. (Saladin allowed Christians continued use of the shrine. Amazingly, the keys of the church are still kept by a local Muslim family.)

The bell tower on the left was originally five-and-a-half storeys high, but was reduced in the eighteenth century, for reasons of safety, to the three storeys visible today. Just outside the picture, on the right, a steep flight of steps leads up to the site known as Golgotha. Approximately 15 feet above ground level, it is covered with a marble pavement to prevent pieces of the rock from being chipped off as souvenirs.

The tomb itself was destroyed in 1009 by order of the mad Caliph al-Hakim and the original burial place in the Rotunda is now enclosed by an elaborate edicule, built in the nineteenth century. The tomb is presumed to have been a typical Jewish grave of the first century (compare the description for the tomb of Annas the High Priest, p. 22)—a vestibule leading into a chamber in which kokhim were cut to receive the body. Fragments of a rolling stone used to close the tomb are said to be kept on a pedestal in the vestibule. Numerous additional chapels and shrines on different levels cluster around the main body of the church, jealously guarded by clergy of various sects.

What is the site's claim to authenticity?

The entrance to the Church of the Holy Sepulchre.

57

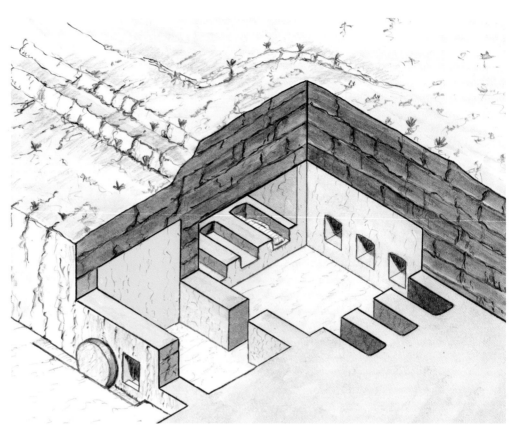

Schematic diagram of a typical family burial cave from the first century A.D. The rock-hewn forecourt (lower left) leads to the entrance of the burial cave, through a narrow opening closed by a rolling or blocking stone.

The Tomb of Jesus, or edicule, in the rotunda of the Holy Sepulchre.

According to the evangelists, the site of the crucifixion was outside yet near the city walls, and it was called Golgotha, meaning "place of a skull." The place of burial was a new tomb belonging to a wealthy disciple called Joseph of Arimathea. A rolling stone was used to close the tomb, which was located in a nearby garden.

Determining the course of the city wall of this period is crucial. As the Church of the Holy Sepulchre stands well inside today's city walls, this fact was often leveled against its genuineness by those who were ignorant of the wall's original course. Excavations carried out in the area reveal that in the early first century A.D., this site was part of a disused quarry containing numerous tombs in the style of the period. As the dead were always buried outside the city, this alone would indicate that the area was not then included within the city walls.

In addition, some fortified remains found in the northern part of the Jewish Quarter excavations have been identified with the Gennath (Garden) Gate mentioned by Josephus. This gate probably derived its name from either a natural or manmade garden situated in the quarry, just to the north, outside the gate. This is corroborated by the Fransciscan archaeologist Virgilio Corbo, who reports finding a layer of arable soil above the quarry fill. In the Jewish Quarter excavations, a wall was found oriented northward, in conformity with Josephus' writings about the Second Wall running north from the Gennath Gate.

Because of the existence of tombs to the west, the most logical course the wall could take was above the eastern rockscarp of the quarry, discovered under both the Church of the Holy Sepulchre and the German Church of the Redeemer. Thus the site could be said to fulfill the main requirements of being outside the walls, close to the city, and in a cultivated area.

The claim that the site could have been known as "the place of the skull" rests on a very different interpretation of this name than that on which the alternative site (below) is based. Here the name is based on an ancient Jewish tradition, reported by early Christian writers such as Origen and Epiphanius, that the skull of Adam, our common ancestor, is preserved in this hill. A chapel called by his name lies beneath the small Church of Golgotha.

Further proof that this is indeed the true site is alleged from the circumstances relating to its discovery in the fourth century. At a time when the early Christians were desperately seeking sites that could be associated with the life of Christ, in order to strengthen their faith, this site was shown by members of the local community to Queen Helena the mother of Constantine, the first Christian Emperor. It would appear that, as early as 326 A.D., tradition firmly had it that the tomb of Jesus was located here. Constantine, for one, was sufficiently convinced to go ahead and build a church in what must have seemed a highly unlikely spot. At that time, the site was covered by a pagan temple which had been constructed by the Roman Emperor Hadrian amidst a busy urban area. Today, a similar leap of the imagination is required to see, behind the facade of the Church of the Holy Sepulchre, a rocky hill where Christ died on the cross between the two thieves and the pastoral setting of his rock-cut tomb.

Skull or Golgotha Hill

Although others, such as the German scholar Otto Thenius (1842) and Claude Conder of the Palestine Exploration Fund (1879) had raised the possibility that the so-called Skull Hill was to be identified as Golgotha, it was General Charles Gordon who first suggested that the two are one and the same.

This theory was proposed in 1883, when the already legendary war hero was on a year's leave of absence from the military in the Holy Land. Before the year

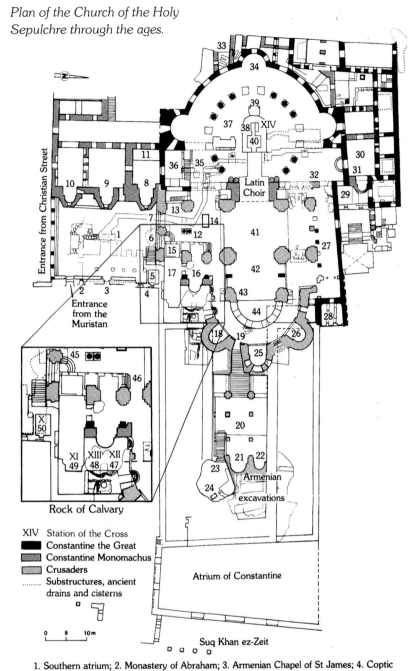

Plan of the Church of the Holy Sepulchre through the ages.

XIV Station of the Cross
■ Constantine the Great
▨ Constantine Monomachus
▦ Crusaders
⋯⋯ Substructures, ancient drains and cisterns

Rock of Calvary

Atrium of Constantine

Suq Khan ez-Zeit

1. Southern atrium; 2. Monastery of Abraham; 3. Armenian Chapel of St James; 4. Coptic Chapel of St Michael the Archangel; 5. Chapel of St Mary of Egypt; 6. Tomb of Philippe d'Aubigny; 7. Main door; 8. Chapel of the Forty Martyrs; 9. Chapel of St Mary Magdalen; 10. Greek Chapel of St James; 11. Belfry; 12. Tomb of Godfrey de Bouillon; 13. Bench for Muslim doorkeepers; 14. Stone of Anointing; 15. Greek Sacristy; 16. Chapel of Adam; 17. Greek Treasury; 18. Chapel of the Derision; 19. Stairway and carved pilgrims' crosses; 20. Crusader Chapel of St Helena (now Armenian Chapel of St Gregory the Illuminator); 21. Altar of St Gregory; 22. Altar of St Dismas; 23. Chapel of the Finding of the Cross; 24. Statue of St Helena; 25. Chapel of the Parting of the Raiment; 26. Chapel of St Longinus; 27. Arches of the Virgin; 28. Prison of Christ; 29. Latin Sacristy; 30. Chapel of the Apparition; 31. Column of Flagellation; 32. Chapel of St Mary Magdalen; 33. Tombs of Joseph of Arimathaea and Nicodemus; 34. Chapel of St Nicodemus (Syrian Orthodox); 35. Place of the Three Maries; 36. Armenian divan; 37. Rotunda; 38. Edicule of the Holy Sepulchre; 39. Coptic Chapel; 40. Chapel of the Angel; 41. 'Navel' of the World; 42. Greek Choir (Katholikon); 43. Throne of the Patriarch of Jerusalem; 44. Altar; 45, 46. Stairs up to Calvary; 47. Greek Altar of the Crucifixion; 48. Latin Altar of *Stabat Mater*; 49. Latin Altar of the Nailing to the Cross; 50. Latin Chapel of the Franks

The so-called Golgotha (Skull) Hill, located just outside the present-day Old City walls, near the Damascus Gate in the northern section of the city. Today the site lies at the back of the main East Jerusalem Bus Station with a Muslim cemetery called es-Sahira located on the hilltop.

was over, he was recalled to the Sudan where he was killed after a nine-month-long siege of Khartoum.

He is said to have made his identification of what would afterwards be known as Gordon's Calvary on the roof of the original American Colony house on the Old City walls just above Solomon's Quarries. He discerned in the contours of the hill opposite the shape of a skull. Others would add that the facial features of a skull—two caves for eyesockets with the rock between them as a nose, could be seen in the rock face which was traditionally known as Jeremiah's Grotto. Continuing the analogy, he visualized the whole of Mount Moriah as a human skeleton with the skull here in the northern position in relation to the Temple Mount, which represented the pelvis. This he took as confirmation that this was indeed the "place of the skull" associated with Christ's crucifixion, in fulfillment of the Scriptural type that the blood of the

sacrifices was always shed on the north side of the altar (Lev. 1.11).

His conclusions, published in a short report in the *PEF Quarterly Statement* two years after his death, caused a storm of controversy. However, because of his heroic last stand at Khartoum and the subsequent identification of a cave in the western scarp of this hill as the tomb of Jesus, his theory, although lacking the weight of scientific proof, gained a large number of adherents, mostly among British Protestants. In support of his theory, Gordon had mentioned the Jewish tradition that placed here the Beit ha-Sekilah or "Place of Stoning" where transgressors were stoned to death.

Independently, the nearby St. Stephen's Church had been built in commemoration of the stoning of Stephen, assuming that because he was stoned to death a short while after the crucifixion of Jesus, the same site of execution would have been used.

The traditional grotto of Jeremiah, as depicted in a 19th century engraving, and which eventually became known as Gordon's Calvary. The excitement which accompanied the hill's discovery is easier to understand if we can mentally remove the modern-day intrusions and see the site as did the nineteenth-century scholars of Jerusalem—an open field where sheep grazed outside the city and, in the background, a rocky crag, with the distinct features of a skull.

The Garden Tomb

The so-called Garden Tomb had already been discovered in 1867 by a local farmer and described by Conrad Schick. Initially, the finding of this tomb, which was similar to many others found in Jerusalem, did not attract much interest. However, Gordon's landmark equation of the hill on which it was located with the site of the crucifixion, called for a re-examination of the tomb. Thus, Gordon's Calvary or Tomb soon became the Garden Tomb.

A group of British Protestants purchased the site in 1894 and formed the Garden Tomb Association "for the preservation of the Tomb outside the walls of Jerusalem, believed by many to be the sepulchre and garden of Joseph of Arimathea...that it might be kept sacred as a quiet spot...."

The tomb comprises an entrance chamber adjoined to a burial chamber. The burial chamber, to the right of the entrance room, originally had burial benches with stone headrests on three walls. This tomb style is totally at variance with the kind that prevailed in the Second Temple period, when the burial chamber or chambers were usually located behind the entrance chamber and not adjoining it like this one. Another important difference is that during the latter period, burial took place in a specially designed niche called a *kokh*, which was cut at right angles into the walls of the tomb or temporarily in an arcosolium, that is, an arched-over burial shelf, and not on benches of the type cut into this tomb.

Because of the wealth of knowledge recently accumulated about the burial customs of various periods, Israeli archaeologists have been able to prove that this tomb was in fact a typical tomb of the First Temple period. They concluded that it formed part of a vast cemetery, dating from the days of the Judean kings (8th–7th centuries B.C.), located to the north of the Damascus Gate. Thus, even if the tomb had been re-used in the Second Temple period, it could not be said to be "new" (John 19.41). During the Byzantine period, the burial benches were cut to create sarcophagi *(right)* The Garden Tomb, in the western escarpment of the hill identified by General Gordon as Golgotha. The rectangular entranceway is thought to originally have been smaller.

(below) Interior view of the Garden Tomb. The visitor would step into the rectangular entrance chamber that measures 10 by 7 feet and 6 feet high (3.05 by 2.15 m and 1.83 m high). Turning right, he would then view the burial chamber itself, which originally had stone benches for laying out the bodies of the deceased. This tomb style is in complete contrast to that of the Second Temple period, an example of which we have seen in the tomb of Annas the High Priest.

and Christian symbols painted on the walls. (No evidence was found of any use of the tomb between the eighth century B.C. and the fifth century A.D.).

The rock surface in front of the cave was lowered during the Crusader period, when the area of the tomb was used as a stable. The large cistern, to support the theory that a garden existed here in the first century, also appears to have been hewn in the Crusader period.

Considering the religious climate in Jerusalem at the end of the nineteenth century, one can appreciate the reason for the popularity of Gordon's proposal among British Protestants. At that time, as now, the Church of the Holy Sepulchre was located in the midst of the bustling Old City with its separate sections contentiously guarded by the various churches. Protestants were not allowed to pray at this shrine, which by its very nature was repellent to them; it should be remembered that of the tomb originally shown in the Holy Sepulchre as the Tomb of Jesus, not one recognizable fragment remained! They were therefore very receptive to suggestions that the authentic site of the crucifixion, burial and resurrection of Christ was elsewhere.

For this reason, the site of the Garden Tomb is still venerated by many as the

true tomb of Jesus. Away from the city hubbub, the tranquillity of a walled garden provides a spot conducive to prayer and meditation concerning the

last days of Christ as described in the Gospels. In addition, the location of the tomb, which represents the sacrifice of Christ, north of the Temple Mount, conforms more than does the Holy Sepulchre with the requirement in Levitical law that the blood be shed on the north side of the altar.

In the time of Jesus, Jerusalem was surrounded by a vast necropolis, or city of the dead, on the north, east and south. Some of the tombs date from the period of the Judean Monarchy and from the post–Babylonian Exile. During the Hellenistic and Hasmonean periods more elaborate tombs were constructed. However, the greatest expansion of these cemeteries took place during the Herodian period—800 tombs were discovered within a radius of 3 miles (5 km) around the city limits of the time.

Jesus, on his walks around Jerusalem to places like Siloam, the Mount of Olives and Bethesda, must have often reflected on the contrast between the beauty of these tombs and the dissolution they represented. He expressed this to the Scribes and Pharisees of his day, "for ye are like unto whited sepulchres, which indeed appear beautiful outward, but are

Three large tombs from the early first century A.D.—from left to right, Absalom's Pillar, the Tomb of Hezir's Priestly Family, and the Tomb of Zechariah—located in the Kedron Valley of today, on the lower slopes of the Mount of Olives opposite the eastern wall of Herod's Temple Mount.
This view has changed little over 2,000 years, apart from the modern Jewish cemetery, lying above these tombs, and the Jerusalem-Jericho road running across the top. This is one of the very few sites in modern-day Jerusalem where the landscape has remained almost identical to that viewed by passers-by in the first century A.D.

within full of dead men's bones and of all uncleanness" (Matt. 23.27).

Many of the tombs were simple, distinguished from the outside only by a small opening, while others were very elaborate. The three tomb complexes shown here include the best preserved monument remaining from this period, known as the Pillar of Absalom. The name commemorates David's rebellious son Absalom, who is said to have reared up a monument for himself here in the King's Dale (2 Sam. 18.18). During the fourth century A.D., the Pilgrim of Bordeaux referred to it as the Tomb of Hezekiah. The identity of the real builder

The Pillar of Absalom.

of the tomb is unknown. The monument is free-standing, with the lower square structure cut out of the rock, containing a burial chamber with arcosolia. The upper part is a circular structure built of finely cut stone, surmounted by a conical structure hewn from a single stone. Prof. Nahman Avigad, who closely examined these tombs, regards the variegated architec-tural style used in their decoration as a mixture of Egyptian and Hellenistic. Parallels have been found at Petra in Jordan.

To the left of the Pillar of Absalom is an eight-chambered catacomb (not visible in the photograph). Its original frieze, adorned with a relief of carved acanthus leaves and fruit, is in a fine state of preservation. As the two tombs were cut at the same time, it is believed that the so-called Pillar of Absalom acted as a monument for the catacomb that was named the Cave of Jehoshaphat. Based on the style, these tombs have

The inscription reads (bottom right of drawing):

וח קברוהנצ ×* לא×לעורהנתחעוריהודח שמעון וחן
כזיוסנכןעזרויוסנואלעור כטחנח
חט×םנכטחוור

The Tomb of Hezir's Priestly Family (cross section) and the Tomb of Zechariah. The inscription (bottom left of drawing) that was found on the tomb of the priestly family reads: "This is the tomb and the monument of Alexander, Hanniah, Yo'ezer, Judah, Simon, Johanan, the sons of Joseph son of Oved. Joseph and Eliezer sons of Hanniah—priests of the Hezir family."

been ascribed to the early part of the first century A.D., when Jesus may well have witnessed their construction.

The tomb in the middle—known as the Tomb of Hezir's Priestly Family (in Hebrew, Bnei [the sons of] Hezir)—is approximately one hundred years older than the Pillar of Absalom. Unlike the tombs which flank it, the name of this tomb is not based on changing traditions, but on a Hebrew inscription carved on the lintel above its entrance. The inscription states that the tomb and its monument belong to the sons of Hezir, a name known from 1 Chronicles 24.15 as the seventeenth of the priestly courses of the Temple. The tomb facade is pure Doric—two Doric columns supporting a Doric frieze, contrary to the composite style used in the nearby tombs. Inside is a porch and a series of burial chambers. Evidence of a former monument is visible to the left of the tomb, where the wall

could have supported a small pyramid.

The Pilgrim of Bordeaux described the tomb on the right as a "true monolith" and believed it to be the tomb of Isaiah. Today it is called the Tomb of Zechariah because of a vision contained in the biblical book of the same name: the appearance of the Messiah and the resurrection of the dead at the time of an earthquake on the Mount of Olives. This association made the surrounding area a favored burial spot for Jews in later periods. The tomb is indeed freestanding, cut out of the surrounding rock and comprises a cube decorated with Ionic pilasters surmounted by a pyramid. A corridor and steps connect this monument with the Tomb of Hezir's Priestly Family. A small chamber, which may have been used as a tomb, is cut out of the rock at the base of the facade. Like Absalom's Pillar, this too has been dated to the early first century A.D.

THE GARDEN OF GETHSEMANE

The Garden of Gethsemane is where Christ suffered before his crucifixion. The site identified with it lies at the foot of the Mount of Olives, which, because of its magnificent views and association with the life of Christ, is today dotted with churches. The mount itself forms a kind of verdant shield protecting the city's inhabitants from the desert beyond. It was, of course, named for the groves of olive trees which grew on its slopes. The name Gethsemane is derived from the Hebrew Gath Shemen, or "Oil Press."

In 1861, the Fransciscans bought a piece of land close to the road leading from the Temple to the top of the Mount of Olives, a likely site for the "agony in the garden." In 1924, the same Franciscan order built the Church of All Nations, so named because church donations from many nations paid for its construction. The building of this church, whose official name is the Basilica of the Agony, reduced the size of the olive garden and covered over the remains of two earlier churches. As in the earliest church, built during the Byzantine period, the Rock of the Agony, on which Jesus is believed to have knelt in prayer, is the central feature. Despite the artificial nature of the present-day garden, the site has a strong claim to authenticity.

The Garden of Gethsemane. Eight ancient olive trees remain here which some botanists claim to be 2,000 years old.

It is unlikely, however, that they date from the time of Christ, as most of the trees then were used to build the Roman siege wall of 70 A.D. Instead they are probably the shoots of trees that flourished here during the first century. Their fine state of preservation is due to the solicitous care given them by Christians throughout the ages. When needed, expert botanists are called in to treat any ailing trees.

The Mount of Olives, looking southeast. In the foreground, the Church of All Nations, or Basilica of the Agony, is the traditional site for the "agony in the garden." However, we can better set the scene for the reading of the Gospel record of Jesus' agony (Matt. 26.36–46; Luke 22.39–46) under the not-so-ancient trees on the slope across the road from the Franciscan olive garden (at the bottom left of the picture,

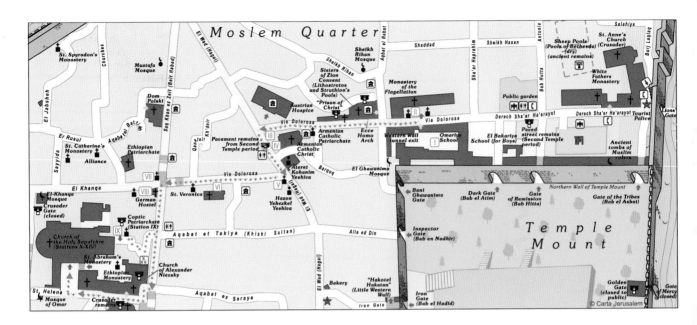

An elaborate system for following the Way of the Cross has been laid out by the Catholic Church. This Via Dolorosa, with its fourteen stations, begins at the Omariyya School, site of the Antonia Fortress, assuming that to be the Praetorium, and ends inside the Church of the Holy Sepulchre.

Ancient olive trees in the Garden of Gethsemane.

70

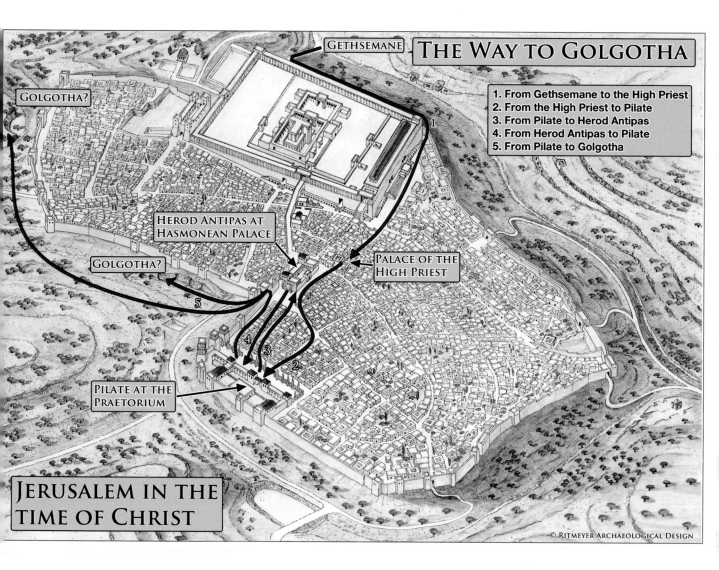

THE WAY TO GOLGOTHA

1. From Gethsemane to the High Priest
2. From the High Priest to Pilate
3. From Pilate to Herod Antipas
4. From Herod Antipas to Pilate
5. From Pilate to Golgotha

GOLGOTHA?

HEROD ANTIPAS AT
HASMONEAN PALACE

GOLGOTHA?

PALACE OF THE
HIGH PRIEST

PILATE AT THE
PRAETORIUM

JERUSALEM IN THE
TIME OF CHRIST

© RITMEYER ARCHAEOLOGICAL DESIGN

A more reasonable way, although it cannot be proven, is to begin at the Upper Room, which, from the description of the "man bearing a pitcher of water" (Luke 22.10), is likely to be near the Water Gate in the Lower City, above the old Gihon Spring. From here Jesus crossed the Kedron Valley, suffered in the garden of Gethsemane and was betrayed. Arrested by the Roman soldiers who had come from the Antonia Fortress, he was led again into the city via a gate located somewhere near the Bethesda Pools (not marked on the reconstruction drawing as its location has not been proven, although it can be deduced, as passage across the Temple Mount through its eastern gate was forbidden). He was first taken to the Palace of the

High Priest, which we have tentatively identified with the Palatial Mansion and then to the Praetorium, which was located in Herod's former Palace. Crossing the streets of the Upper City to the old Hasmonean Palace, he was questioned and mocked by Herod Antipas and his men, who then sent him back to Pilate in the Praetorium. After being condemned he was led to his crucifixion "without the gate" to Golgotha (here one must choose between the two alternative sites).

Five stages in Christ's last journey can be identified, beginning at Gethsemane and culminating at either of the two sites identified as the place of the empty tomb. (See key on drawing.)

71

General view of Jerusalem, looking south.

Although some of the landmarks of Jerusalem of the first century A.D. remain tantalizingly elusive, we have learned enough of its make-up to allow us to open a door into this historical world. We see that many of the sites mentioned in the Gospels and in Acts lie exactly where the Bible places them and we are led to perceive how firmly the Word is rooted in the actuality of the Land. Josephus may sometimes have been prone to exaggeration, but an investigation of the sites he so painstakingly describes, infuses a sense of vividness into the study of his narrative that reading alone cannot provide. Many of the sites today are totally different from what they once were and physical contact with them can actually be a distraction. Yet even these sites, by compelling us to exercise our imagination, help to expand the scope of our understanding.